UN Peace Operations

Part V

Women, Peace and Security

UN Peace Operations

Part V

Women, Peace and Security

Edited by

A K Bardalai and Pradeep Goswami

(Established 1870)

A Joint USI - ICWA Publication

Vij Books India Pvt Ltd
New Delhi (India)

Published by

Vij Books India Pvt Ltd
(Publishers, Distributors & Importers)
2/19, Ansari Road
Delhi – 110 002
Phones: 91-11-43596460
Mob: 98110 94883
e-mail: contact@vijpublishing.com
web : www.vijbooks.in

First Published in India in 2022

ISBN: 978-93-93499-86-8

Contents

Special Commentary

Closing Remarks

Major General BK Sharma, AVSM, SM & Bar (Retd)

Preface

It has been close to seven decades since the deployment of the first UN peace operations - United Nations Emergency Force in Gaza in 1956. The strategy that was followed by Dag Hammarskjold, the second Secretary-General to employ the peacekeeping contingents later laid the framework for subsequent peace operations. The principles of peacekeeping - consent, impartiality, and minimum use of force formed the core of the Secretary-General's strategy. Even though Hammarskjold did not visualise the use of force for intervention operations, he did anticipate the blurring line between the use of force in self-defence and combat operations under Chapter VI, as it would be seen later in Congo in the 1960s. As the UN operations evolved and the conflicts became more intra-state, the peacekeeping missions were mandated with multi-functional and difficult tasks. In the year 2021, The United Services Institution (USI) of India, a leading independent think tank of India, with support from the Indian Council of World Affairs (ICWA), planned and conducted a series of webinars on UN peace operations as under:

a) **27 February 2021**. India and UN Peace Operations: Principles of UN Peacekeeping and Mandates (https://usiofindia.org/wp-content/uploads/2022/01/Monograph-Principals-of-Peacekeeping-Mandate.pdf).

b) **29 June 2021**. UN Peace Operations: Hostage-taking of UN Peacekeepers (https://usiofindia.org/wp-content/uploads/2022/01/Monograph_Hostage-Taking-of-Peacekeepers.pdf).

c) **25 August 2021**. Effectiveness of UN Peace Operations: Dynamics of Composition of Troops and Diversity of UN Peace Operations (https://usiofindia.org/wp-content/uploads/2022/01/UN-Monograph-Part-III-Effectiveness.pdf).

d) **22 October 2021**. UN Peace Operations: Protection of Civilians (https://usiofindia.org/wp-content/uploads/2022/01/UN-Peacekeeping-Part-IV_-PoC.pdf)

In intra-state conflicts, the civilian population suffers the most. Hence, the protection of civilians has become the core mandated task for almost all peace operations. In this regard, the way women and children even though are civilians, suffer in the conflict is worse than the male. Despite guidelines from the UN, protecting civilians faces several challenges and women continue to suffer. In a civil war, women are not only subjected to a physical threat to their lives but also are subjected to gender discrimination and sexual harassment. In some cases, violence against women has become the political agenda for intervention by force and to humiliate the opponents. Discussions and debates on Women, Peace, and Security (WPS) generally conclude with recommendations that, if implemented, can provide a long-term solution to the challenges to WPS.

The policy guidelines and strategies to provide protection to women in the conflict are evolving. Member states, Troop Contributing Countries (TCC), scholars, and academicians are generally in agreement with the current policy and the strategy. However, these documents are absent of workable recommendations to provide physical protection in the field. Like any other policy guideline, there is a huge gap between the theories and their practices. Probably because of this reason and lacking faith in the UN to provide protection, women may take the risk of protecting themselves like the way several Afghan women come to the streets defying the Taliban.

To understand how the threat to women differs from that of other civilians, its challenges, and how best the peacekeeping missions can reorient to provide better security to this vulnerable community, this webinar focused on the following sub-themes:

a) An overview of the WPS and challenges – the perspective of an academician.

b) Peculiar challenges to protecting women in the conflict zone – experiences of a peacekeeper from the field.

c) Challenges to protecting women in the conflict zone and recommendations to mitigate the threat – views of a practitioner (Blue Helmet).

While the last webinar focused on the protection of civilians, this webinar discussed the complexity of the protection of only women. It was a women's event wherein the participants brought with them their individual rich experiences from the academic field as well as the conflict zone.

This monograph is a compilation of talks by eminent speakers during the webinar as well as reminiscences of peace keeper and executive on 'UN Peace Operations: Women, Peace, and Security'.

About the Participants

Major General BK Sharma, AVSM, SM (Retd)** is the Director of the United Service Institution (USI) of India. He has tenanted prestigious assignments in India, including command of a mountain division on the China border and Senior Faculty Member at the National Defence College, New Delhi. He represented his country at the UN as Military Observer in Central America and has been India's Defence Attaché in Central Asia. He specialises in Strategic Net Assessment methodology, Scenario Building and Strategic Gaming.

Amb Vijay Thakur Singh is the Director-General, Indian Council of World Affairs (ICWA). She is a carrier diplomat and had multilateral experience during her service with the Ministry of External Affairs, GOI. She was High Commissioner of India to Singapore and Ireland and prior to that, Joint Secretary to the President of India and Joint Secretary at the National Security Council Secretariat. She also handled Afghanistan and Pakistan desk in the Ministry of External Affairs and was Counsellor in the Embassy of India in Kabul. She was also a Counsellor in the Permanent Mission of India to the United Nations in New York. She retired in Sept 2020 as Secretary (East), Ministry of External Affairs.

Major General PK Goswami, VSM (Retd) is the Deputy Director, USI and Head USI-UN Cell. He represented his country at the UN as an Unarmed Military Observer with United Nations Verification Mission at Angola (UNAVEM) in

1991-92. He was also the Senior Faculty Member at National Defence College, New Delhi. He represented National Defence College, India at the 16th ASEAN Regional Forum for Heads of Defence Universities, Colleges and Institutions in Beijing, China in Nov 2012.

Dr Yeshi Choedon is a professor at the Centre for International Politics, Organisation and Disarmament, School of International Studies, JNU, New Delhi. Her research interests include peace, security, democratisation and human rights. Earlier she was a Lecturer and later as Reader at the Sikkim Government College, Gangtok. She was awarded the UGC Career Award and was a DAAD Fellow at Free University, Berlin in 1997. As an awardee of Nehru-Fulbright Senior Research Fellowship, she was affiliated with University of Illinois, USA. She has authored two books, number of chapters in edited volumes, number of research articles in national and international journals.

Dr Tasneem Meenai is Professor and former Director, Nelson Mandela Centre for Peace and Conflict Resolution, Jamia Millia Islamia, New Delhi. Her areas of research and interest are Humanitarian Dimensions of Armed Conflict, Multilateral Institutions and Conflict Resolution, United Nations Peacekeeping, Peace-making and Peace Building. She earlier worked as Research Fellow at the Institute for Defence Studies and Analyses (IDSA) on the research project titled "Role of Multilateral Institutions in Conflict Resolution". She co-edited 'United Nations, Multilateralism and International Security' and co-authored 'Iraq War 2003 – Rise of the New Unilateralism'.

Lieutenant Colonel VM Hanrahan is a Military Police Officer in the Canadian Forces. She commanded the Canadian Forces National Investigation Support Detachment and was Executive Assistant to the Canadian Forces Provost Marshal.

In August 2010, she was deployed in Afghanistan for a year as Officer Commanding, Canadian Afghan Uniform Police Training team, helping develop the Afghan National Police in the Province of Kandahar. In 2018-2019 she was Special Advisor to the Canadian Forces Provost Marshal, and then deployed in support of the UN Mission in South Sudan as the Task Force Provost Marshal, a position she held until November 2020. She is presently pursuing second language training (French) at Ottawa.

Commandant Poonam Gupta is presently commanding 232 (Mahila) Bn, CRPF. Earlier she was with Rapid Action Force (RAF) and VIP Security. She was Chief Operational Officer of first batch of all female Indian Female Police Unit (IFPU) for Liberia in 2007 and subsequently Contingent Commander for IFPU in 2011. IFPU's major achievement was the successful conduct of the Presidential election in Liberia and bringing Liberia women into security sector in the capacity of mentors and trainers.

DIG Seema Dhundia, presently DIG with RAF Sector, CRPF and looking after the administration and operations of 15 Bns. She has numerous firsts to her credit: joined CRPF in 1987 in first batch of lady officers, raising of first All-Female Battalion in CRPF, Contingent Commander of first All-Female Formed Police Unit in the history of UN deployed in Liberia in 1997. She is a recipient of Police Medal for Meritorious Service and the Presidents Police Medal for Distinguished Service.

Major Suman Gawani of the Indian Army served as a peacekeeper with the United Nations Mission in South Sudan (UNMISS) and was the focal point of contact for gender-related issues for the mission. She participated and encouraged participation in joint military patrols to maintain the gender balance. She supported the UNMISS

Force initiative and trained the government forces of South Sudan on CRSV related aspects, and helped them to launch their action plan on CRSV. She is a recipient of the prestigious United Nations Military Gender Advocate of the year 2019 award.

Ms Sangya Malla is a medical professional and Superintendent of Police (SP) of Nepal Police Force. Presently she is serving in UNPOL, in MONUSCO, at Goma, Congo (DRC). She established the unit, responsible for implementing policies and procedures concerning the health and well-being of personnel as well as United Nations Police environmental initiatives. Her contributions have been especially important during the ongoing COVID-19 pandemic, past Ebola outbreaks, and natural and humanitarian crises such as the volcanic eruption in the city of Goma. Earlier she served as medical team in Haiti. She is recipient of the UN Woman Police Officer of the Year Award for 2021.

Colonel (Dr) KK Sharma (Retd) was a military observer in UNTAC, Cambodia in 1992 - 1993. He was an active member in planning and writing of UN Capstone Doctrine on peacekeeping and manuals for trainers in the Office of High Commissioner of Human Rights, Geneva. He has been associated with the planning cell of peacekeeping operations in Army HQ and was a founding member of starting Centre for UN Peacekeeping under the USI of India. He is PhD in Management from Zurich, Switzerland, and is presently associated with Global Education Programs in Chitkara University as a Professor.

Amb Lakshmi Puri is former Assistant Secretary-General UN and Deputy Executive Director, UN Women; and was India's Ambassador to Hungary concurrently accredited to Bosnia and Herzegovina. Prior to her 15 year stint at the United Nations, she served as an Indian diplomat for 28 years in MEA,

GOI. She is recipient of the prestigious Eleanor Roosevelt Human Rights Award, Novus Award for Championing the Sustainable Development Goals, the Millennium Campus Award 2015 and Global Generation Award as Inspiration for Youth; for her work and contribution. She is a Distinguished Fellow of Indian Association of International Studies (IAIS), and has several publications and Op-eds to her credit.

Concept Note

UN Peace Operations: Women, Peace and Security

Along with the decline in inter-state conflicts and a sharp increase in intra-state conflicts in the last two decades, there is a consequent increase in the casualties of innocent civilians. Taking note of this by the international community, S/RES/1265 of 1999 was the first UN resolution mandating peacekeeping missions to protect civilians. That apart, since women and children are the worst victims of war, the UN Security Council adopted the S/RES/1325 on 31 October 2000 setting the agenda for Women, Peace, and Security (WPS). It was followed by the development of the operational concept of Protection of Civilians (PoC) in 2010 and the issue of the first DPKO/DFS Policy on PoC in 2015. The latest policy on PoC (Ref. 2019.17) of 01 November 2019 outlines a comprehensive approach to PoC. The three-tier actions: Protection through dialogue; Provision of physical protection and Establishment of a protective environment are the main tenants of this policy.

However, this policy suffers from ambiguity in its concept and implementation. As a result, the peacekeeping missions often come under criticism for not being able to do enough to protect the civilians. The negative fallout of such ambiguity has further compounded the challenges to women, peace, and security. Whatever little progress would have been made, women continue to suffer. In a civil war, women are not only subjected to a physical threat to their lives but also are subjected to gender discrimination and sexual harassment. In some cases, violence against women has become the political agenda for intervention by force and to humiliate the opponents.

UNSCR 1325 has marked the start of the WPS agenda. Participation of women in peace initiatives, protection from violence, and prevention of conflicts are the main core elements of this agenda. Amongst many, the main reasons for violence against women are gender inequality, discrimination against women, and lack of participation of women in peace initiatives. Implementation of the WPS agenda has both long-term and immediate impacts on the vulnerable community. For instance, unless the very root causes of the threat to women are addressed, and women are empowered to take their rightful place in society, women and children would continue to suffer. The concept, policy, and most discussions on WPS, however, revolve around the long-term and sustainable approach to the protection of women. What, however, is absent is the concrete guidance on how the immediate threat to the women can be mitigated by the peacekeepers. It is not to reject the idea of the crucial role of women either in the prevention of cruelty to women or peace initiatives. The participation of women in peacekeeping itself could be a deterrence against committing crimes, fearing the impact of their testimony in the subsequent investigations. Besides, women victims would also be more open to telling their stories to a woman peacekeeper. Similarly, reform of the security sector and prevention of the use of arms by the process of DDR, and a ban on illegal arms are some of the measures that can make long-term contributions to giving a shape to the idea of protection of women.

At the same time, when it comes to the peacekeepers implementing the PoC mandate, it boils down to preventing or mitigating the physical threat to the woman. While the structural changes are important, providing physical protection to the women in the conflict zone is something that can bring immediate relief to victims as well as credibility and local legitimacy to the peace operations. For instance, when the government forces of South Sudan stormed Hotel Terrain in July 2016 and physically abused (including rape) the women employees of the UN, and UNMISS did not come to their rescue until almost everything was over, would the presence of women peacekeepers have helped to prevent the situation? The question, therefore, is how the threat to women differs from that to other civilians, what are the challenges and how best the peacekeeping missions can reorient to provide better security to this vulnerable community. Or is there no new way to provide protection to the vulnerable community other than making structural changes as given out in the WPS agenda? This webinar would focus on the following sub-themes:

- ➤ An overview of the WPS and challenges – the perspective of an academician.

- ➤ Peculiar challenges to protecting women in the conflict zone – experiences of a civilian peacekeeper from the field.

- ➤ Challenges to protecting women in the conflict zone and recommendations to mitigate the threat – views of a practitioner (Blue Helmet).

Introductory Remarks

Major General PK Goswami, VSM (Retd)

On behalf of Maj Gen BK Sharma, Director, USI and Amb Vijay Thakur Singh, Director General, ICWA, I welcome all participants to today's webinar.

I am glad to inform all that since 2021, the USI, in collaboration with ICWA is conducting a series of webinars on UN-related issues. The inaugural webinar was held on 27 February 2021 on **'Principles of UN Peace Keeping and Mandate'**, followed by **'The Impact of Climate Change on UN Peacekeeping Operations'** on 20 April 2021 in collaboration with NUPI & SIPRI; **'UN Peace Operations: Hostage-taking of UN Peacekeepers'** on 29 June 21 and **'Effectiveness of UN Peace Operations'** with focus on **'Dynamics of Composition of Troops and Diversity on UN Peace Operations'** on 25 August 2021. Today is the fifth one and will deliberate on **'UN Peace Operations'** with a focus on **'Women, Peace, and Security'**, this is in continuation of our last webinar on Protection of Civilians.

At the conclusion of each webinar, all talks are being compiled and printed as a Monograph, to share the rich experience of speakers, with a larger audience and cross-fertilisation of ideas. I am glad to inform you that the Monograph of our last (fourth) webinar on Protection of Civilians has been published. Today's webinar on **'Women,**

Peace, and Security' will be more focused since all the lead speakers are ladies.

I express my deep gratitude to Dr Yeshi Choedon, Dr. Tasneem Meenai, Lt Col Vanessa Hanarahan, Commandant Poonam Gupta, DIG Seema Dhundia, Maj Suman Gawani, and Ms Sangya Malla, for accepting my request to share their rich experience and deep insight on Women, Peace, and Security. They will be introduced by the moderator as we proceed further with the webinar. We are also fortunate to have a galaxy of UN professionals and practitioners, and friends from Turkey, Bangladesh, Nepal, Sri Lanka, and S Korea participating in the event today. Before we proceed further, a few words about today's theme – Women, Peace, and Security.

Armed conflict affects women, men, girls, and boys in different ways. Women and girls face discrimination based on their gender and displaced women and refugees are especially vulnerable to conflict-related sexual violence. At the same time, women and girls play a key role in preserving their communities, and in turn, their economic and social responsibilities may increase in times of conflict. Despite their ability to act as agents of peace, women are often excluded from the process of conflict resolution.

Thus, recognising the disproportionate impact that conflict has on women and girls, the vital roles women play in peace and security, and the importance of incorporating gender perspectives in all the Alliance, the United Nations Security Council unanimously passed Resolution 1325 (UNSCR 1325) on 31 October 2000, and now includes nine additional Resolutions (1820, 1888, 1889, 1960, 2106, 2122, 2422, 2467 and 2493). These resolutions seek to include women at all levels of decision-making and at different stages of the conflict. It also calls for incorporating the needs and concerns of women in relief and recovery efforts. However, this vulnerable community continues to suffer the most because of the absence of a comprehensive strategy to protect them. This is the main theme of today's webinar.

Women peacekeepers obviously serve as powerful mentors and role models for women and girls in post-conflict settings in the host community, being examples for them to advocate for their own rights and pursue non-traditional careers. Thus, UN Security Council has set a target of doubling the number of women in uniformed components of peace operations by 2028, Military Observer & staff officers at 25%, in military contingents at 15%, Police officers at 30%, in police units at 20%, other categories at 30%. Even though remarkable progress has been achieved (in Military officers, Staff officers, or Police officers) since the adoption of the Uniformed Gender Parity Strategy, efforts are still needed (for mil contingents and police units) to reach targets for 2028 and beyond and sustain them those that have been met. In continuation of UN efforts, on 01 February 22, UNIFIL Lebanon was released funds by Canadian Elsie Initiative for Women in Peace Operations to support Women's peacekeeping initiatives.

India has a long tradition of sending women on UN peacekeeping missions because it strongly believes that more women in peacekeeping mean more effective peacekeeping. In fulfilling its commitments; India has a lot to its credit. In 1960 India deployed a team of women from the Indian Armed Forces Medical Services in the UN peacekeeping mission in the Republic of Congo for the setting up of a 400-bed hospital, and medical support has continued in all other missions also. In 2007 India deployed the first-ever all-female Formed Police Unit (FPU) in Liberia, which served for a decade. DIG Seema then Commandant & Commandant Poonam then Chief Operations Officer of the unit, are with us. (They earned the incredible goodwill of locals and encouraged a number of girls to join the national police organisation in Liberia). India was the first country to contribute to the Secretary-General's Trust Fund for Victims of Sexual Exploitation and Abuse (SEA) and also signed the Voluntary Compact between the United Nations and Member States, on SEA in 2017. This includes specific commitments to combat and prevent sexual exploitation and abuse in operational areas. We have also pledged a Women Formed Police Unit (FPU) under the Peacekeeping Readiness Capability System. India deployed Female Engagement Team in the Congo as part of the Rapidly Deployable Battalion in MONUSCO in 2020. India is fully committed to increasing the number of women peacekeepers to the United Nations and meeting the targets in this regard within the specified timelines. But Indian example, unfortunately, still remains a rarity.

Indian efforts have been appreciated, recognised, and also rewarded. During the de-induction of the Indian Formed Police Unit in Feb 2016 from Liberia, President Ellen Johnson-Sirleaf said, and I quote, "We see you as family, If I had my will, I would have recommended for another unit of the United Nations Mission in Liberia (UNMIL) to leave, so that the Indian Formed Police Unit (FPU) would continue its stay in the country for the time being" unquote. Indian Army officer Major Suman Gawani, was awarded the UN Military Gender Advocate of the year for 2019 for her role as a peacekeeper with the UN Mission in South Sudan (UNMISS). Similarly, Ms. Sangya Malla from Nepal Police Force, presently deployed in South Sudan, is the recipient of the UN Woman Police Officer of the Year Award for 2020. And we are fortunate that they will be sharing their experiences with us today.

Ambassador Vijay Thakur Singh has been a carrier diplomat and had multilateral experience, during her service with the Ministry of External Affairs, GOI. She was the High Commissioner of India to Singapore and Ireland. She was also a Counsellor in the Permanent Mission of India to the United Nations in New York. She retired in Sept 2020, as Secretary (East), Ministry of External Affairs. Now Ambassador Vijay Thakur Singh, DG, ICWA (Indian Council of World Affairs) will deliver the Opening Remarks.

Our moderator for the event today is Dr. Yeshi Choedon, who is a professor at the Centre for International Politics, Organisation, and Disarmament, School of International Studies, JNU, New Delhi. Her research interests include peace, security, democratisation, and human rights. She is the recipient of the UGC Career Award and Nehru-Fulbright Senior Research Fellowship. She has authored two books, a number of chapters in edited volumes, and a number of research articles in national and international journals.

Opening Address

UN Peace Operations: Women, Peace & Security

Amb Vijay Thakur Singh

Ladies and gentlemen,

It is a privilege to speak in the presence of such a Distinguished Panel of Speakers, all of who are women achievers in their respective fields – scholars, Officers of the Army, the Para Military, and the Police. With their rich experience, I am confident they would bring valuable insights to the topic of today's webinar: "UN Peace Operations: Women, Peace, and Security".

We are also meeting in the backdrop of the appointment of Amb. Rabab Fatima of Bangladesh as the Chair of the UN Peacebuilding Commission (PBC) – the first woman to be elected to this position. As an intergovernmental advisory body, this Commission supports peace efforts in conflict-affected countries and contributes to the capacity of the international community to further strengthen the peace agenda.

Indeed, the role of gender within the broader ambit of International Relations and Diplomacy needs serious consideration. We in ICWA held a Conference last year on the topic, "Women and Power- Gender within International

Relations and Diplomacy"; and in a subsequent Conference focussed on, 'Gender Sensitive Indian Foreign Policy – How? and Why?'. In the discussions, the need for applying a gender lens to foreign policy issues ranging from peace and security (including peacekeeping) to development partnership and humanitarian assistance was emphasised.

It is well known that violent conflicts disproportionately affect women and girls and intensify gender inequalities and discrimination. Their role in conflict situations as key players and agents of peace is equally important, a fact that must be recognised as well as given prominence.

At the international level, UN Security Council has adopted ten Resolutions on 'Women, Peace and Security' (WPS) with UN Security Council Resolution 1325 at the centre of this agenda. This Resolution highlights the need to engage more women in peacekeeping operations around the world and also affirms the role of women in the prevention, management, and resolution of conflicts, peacebuilding, humanitarian responses, and post-conflict reconstruction. In other words, in the entire spectrum of peace efforts.

Women's roles in UN peacekeeping operations span across police, military and civilian levels. Today, women are playing a greater role in UN peacekeeping operations than in the past and have made a positive impact on peacekeeping environments. In 1993, only one percent of all deployed uniformed personnel in UN peacekeeping were women. In 2020, out of approximately 95,000 peacekeepers, women constituted 4.8% of military contingents and 10.9% of formed police units. A watershed moment occurred in 2014 when Maj Gen Kristin Lund of Norway was appointed as the first female to serve as Force Commander in a UN peacekeeping operation - the UN PKO in Cyprus. The UN Uniformed

Gender Parity Strategy rolled out in 2018, aims to increase women's representation to 35 percent by 2028.

In all fields of peacekeeping, women peacekeepers have proven that they can perform the same roles, to the same standards, and under the same difficult conditions, as their male counterparts. If at all, a larger number of women peacekeepers only leads to protection responses that are more credible and meet the needs of all members of local communities. Studies conducted by the UN in support of Resolution 1325, of experience in operations in Cambodia, Kosovo, Timor-Leste, Afghanistan, Liberia, and DRC, have shown that female soldiers do not face the same cultural restrictions as their male counterparts and are able to gain information from women and children. Lt. Col. Vanessa of the Canadian Army, who is participating in the webinar today, served in Afghanistan; and I am sure that she would have experienced this first hand, as I did, as a diplomat posted in Kabul. This ability to gain the trust of the local population should be considered a vital component of any peacekeeping operation. Further, troop contingents with a larger number of women are credited with lower incidences of sexual exploitation and abuse. We look forward to hearing the experience of Major Suman Gawani, who during her South Sudan Mission has encouraged the participation of joint military patrols to maintain gender balance.

As one of the largest troop contributors to UN peacekeeping missions, India has the distinction of providing the first-ever all-female Formed Police Unit (FPU) for UN Peacekeeping in Liberia. I am sure that Comdt. Poonam Gupta will share her experience as the Chief Operational Officer of this Unit as will DIG Seema Dhundia, who also was deployed with this mission. DIG Seema Dhundia even has to her credit the experience of raising the first all-women battalion in CRPF – India's paramilitary force. India was hailed by the UN for its leadership as this FPU mission successfully demonstrated the 'Participation' of women in conflict management, 'Protection' of women from conflict-related violence, and 'Prevention' of conflict. The then UN Secretary-General Ban Ki-moon only had praised the work of the all-female FPU from India when it ended its mission in Liberia in 2016.

More recently, India deployed a Female Engagement Team in the UN Stabilization Mission in the Democratic Republic of Congo MONUSCO in 2019. Working during the Covid period, was a very trying period globally. Superintendent of Police Sangya Malla of Nepal Police Force was deployed during this period in MONUSCO, at Goma, Congo. In today's discussion, her views and experience would add the dimension of women's role during health emergencies.

In the current global peace and security context and given the ongoing pandemic, the efforts to implement the women, peace, and security agenda are more critical now than ever.

Women peacekeepers and the unique understanding, experiences, and capabilities that they bring to bear on all aspects of UN peace operations are valuable for better peacekeeping.

I look forward to the deliberations today and wish all the speakers of the webinar the very best.

Thank You.

Uniformed Women in UN Peacekeeping Operation: Challenges of Women's Participation

Prof Yeshi Choedon

Introduction

Peacekeeping operation continues to be the main mechanism of maintaining peace and security even as the nature of conflict changed from inter-state to intra-state in the post-Cold War. The intra-state conflict generated a humanitarian crisis with large-scale atrocities on the civilians. This kind of conflict disproportionately affects women and girls and intensifies pre-existing gender inequalities and discrimination. It made them one of the most vulnerable groups in the conflict-affected areas. Although the roles and responsibilities of UN peacekeeping operations have been expanded since 1989 with mandated multi-dimensional functions, the UN Security Council did not give a specific mandate to protect civilians till late 1999. The pressure of the international community compelled the UN Security Council to give a specific mandate for the protection of civilians (POC) for the first time in October 1999 to the UN mission in Sierra Leone. Since then, the POC has become one of the core tasks of the UN peacekeeping operations (Holt and Taylor, 2006: 18).

There was also no specific mandate to protect women in the conflict areas until 2000. In response to gender-blind international responses to conflict, the women's movement and civil society organisations ramped up their efforts to highlight the peculiar vulnerability of women and girls in the intra-state conflict and demanded a gendered approach to the conflict. Particularly, the Beijing conference on women in 1995 demanded mainstreaming of gender into all UN activities, including activities related to security and conflict resolution (UN Women, n). These sensitisation and mobilisation activities made the UN Security Council formally discuss and unanimously adopt resolution 1325 on Women, Peace, and Security (WPS) in October 2000.

It is a wide-ranging resolution that reaffirms the important role of women in conflict prevention and resolution, peace negotiations, peace-building, peacekeeping, humanitarian response, and post-conflict reconstruction. It stresses the importance of women's equal participation and full involvement in all efforts to maintain and promote peace and security. It also urges all stakeholders to take action to increase the participation of women and calls on the UN to incorporate gender perspectives into all of its peace and security efforts.

Importance of Uniformed Women Peacekeepers

Resolution 1325 is considered a ground-breaking achievement as it shifts the attention from women as victims to women as resources. The resolution stresses the importance of women's equal participation and full involvement in all efforts to maintain and promote peace and security. It also highlights an urgent 'need to mainstream gender perspective into peacekeeping operations' (UNSC, 2000). The comprehensive provisions of the Resolution could be roughly grouped into three main categories:

> ➢ The first category of the provision focuses on urging the member states to increase women's representation and active participation at all decision-making levels

relating to conflict prevention, conflict management, conflict resolution, and peacebuilding. This category of the provision aims to promote gender empowerment and gender equality.

> ➢ The second category focuses on the need to include a gender perspective in planning and implementing peace operations and peace negotiations. It attempts to ensure women's voices are heard and taken into account at the highest level.

> ➢ The third category of provision emphasises the need for increased attention to protecting and respecting women's rights, including protection against gender-based violence.

It is clear that apart from protection and participation, the UN is required to ensure that gender perspectives and gender equality are central to all activities. The UN Security Council has cemented its commitment by subsequently adopting nine follow-up resolutions. Women Peace and Security (WPS) Agenda now consists of UN Security Council Resolution 1325 and nine follow-up resolutions. The nine subsequent resolutions on Women, Peace, and Security (1820, 1888, 1889, 1960, 2106, 2122, 2242, 2467, 2493) have stressed the importance of women's leadership and meaningful participation in the prevention and resolution of conflicts; addressing the impact of sexual violence; promoting the development and use of measures and standards for monitoring the implementation of women, peace and security mandates; training and capacity building on gender equality and women, peace and security for peacekeeping personnel; engaging with civil society more comprehensively and enabling an improved understanding of gender dynamics of conflict (The United Nations Peacekeeping, na).

As resolution 1325 specifically calls for the increased participation of women in the UN peacekeeping operations, the UN has issued several numerical targets to increase the number of uniformed women peacekeepers. Both the UN Secretary-General and the Department of Peacekeeping Operations have been urging TCCs/PCCs to deploy more uniformed women peacekeepers. There are several reasons for the need to increase the number of uniformed women in UN peace operations.

One of the most frequent rationales given is women have specific traits which enable them to excel at tasks that men cannot perform. It has been perceived that woman could engage with the local community and women groups more effectively, bringing greater situational awareness and improving intelligence gathering. The local community also finds it easier to interact with women peacekeepers as they are less intimating than men peacekeepers. Moreover, the presence of women peacekeepers is also expected to provide a greater sense of security to local populations and reduce conflict and confrontation (Karim and Beardsley, 2013: 472).

Another often cited reason for the increase in uniformed women's participation in the UN peacekeeping operations is they are regarded as more sensitive to the needs and challenges of the civilians in conflict areas, particularly women and children. Due to their more compassionate or empathetic response, the women peacekeepers are also perceived to be particularly suitable for dealing with female victims of sexual and gender-based violence (SGBV) (Jennings, 2013:3).

Even the UN guideline document claims that mixed patrolling teams are better as "the presence of female military personnel can boost protection and response strategies ... especially in the case of sexual violence" (DPKO/DFS 2010). During a discussion at the UN Security Council, the UN Secretary-General stated, "The presence of more women in troop contingents is also credited with higher reporting of sexual and gender-based violence, as well as lower incidents of sexual exploitation and abuse" (Guterres, 2019). The UN also claims that "Women peacekeepers are essential enablers to build trust and confidence with local communities and help improve access and support for local women, for example, by interacting with women in societies where women are prohibited from speaking to men (United Nations Peacekeeping. nb)."

Another frequently cited reason for increasing uniformed women peacekeepers is that they have a comparative practical advantage in carrying out certain activities, such as house searches, body searches, working in women's prisons, interviewing victims of SGBV, providing escorts for victims/witnesses, and screening women combatants at disarmament, demobilisation, and reintegration (DDR) sites (Karim and Beardsley, 2013: 471). Thus, the increasing number of uniformed women peacekeepers is expected to broaden the skills available within peacekeeping missions.

Another reason for increasing uniformed women peacekeepers is that they serve as powerful inspiration and role models for the local women and girls in the conflict areas to assert their rights in society and pursue non-traditional careers. In this way, the uniformed women peacekeepers promote more equitable gender relations within the local community (United Nations Peacekeeping, nb; Jennings, 2013:4).

Low Number of Uniformed Women Peacekeepers

Despite the solid reasons for increasing the participation of uniformed women peacekeepers for the missions' effectiveness and appeal to the troops and police-contributing countries (TCCs/PCCs) to meet the target set from time to time, there has been an extremely slow rise in the number of uniformed women peacekeepers. In August 2006, when the UN started to record female military participants in UN peacekeeping operations, only 1.85 percent of women participated in the contingent troops (United Nations Peacekeeping, nc). In October 2015, the UN Security Council adopted Resolution 2242, which called for the 'doubling of the numbers of women in military and police contingents of UN peacekeeping operations 'over the next five years' (UNSC, 2015). Despite all efforts to increase the number of uniformed women peacekeepers, women military personnel in UN operations was just 4 percent, women police personnel only 11.35 percent by December 2017 (United Nations Peacekeeping, nd).

Against this backdrop of low participation of the uniformed women peacekeepers, the UN Department of Peacekeeping Operations put forward the Uniformed Gender Parity Strategy of 2018-2028, which set targets for the next decade. It has targeted that by 2028 women should constitute 15 percent of deployed contingent troops, 30 percent of individual police officers, and 20 percent of formed police units (Department of Peace Operations, 2018). These targets seem to be ambitious even to the top TCCs/PCCs.

There are various reasons for the low participation of uniformed women in UN peacekeeping operations. Many of the national security structures of TCCs/PCCs, being male-dominated, see women as needing protection rather than viewing them as providers of protection (Ferrari, 2019). Therefore, they are reluctant to send uniformed women to the UN missions in their contingents. Some authors have argued that TCCs/PCCs may be reluctant to send female peacekeepers as they consider it risky and fear backlash if something happens to them in peacekeeping deployment.

Even those who contribute uniformed women peacekeepers tend to contribute to those operations considered less risky. They avoid sending uniformed women peacekeepers to mission environments associated with high conflict intensity and prevalence of conflict-related sexual violence. Thus, the relative risk of a mission influences the TCCs/PCCs of allocation patterns of uniformed women peacekeepers (Karim and Beardsley, 2013: 469). Some also expressed that the deployment of the uniformed women peacekeepers in low-risk mission environments means that they would not be deployed where the need for a gender perspective is greatest, i.e. where levels of sexual violence are high or gender inequality is particularly rampant (Kreft, 2017:135).

Some have argued that uniformed women peacekeepers are less likely to be deployed in the early stages of missions because new missions are associated with high levels of operational uncertainty and risk. The participation of the uniformed women peacekeepers tends to increase with the decrease in uncertainty and the operating environment becomes more predictable (Tidblad-Lundholm, 2020: 673). Thus, the concept of risk highly influences withholding uniformed women from participation in UN peace operations. This could mean that leaders of TCCs/PCCs are influenced by gender stereotypes, who consider women to be protected rather than deployed in the UN missions as protectors.

Some regard the lack of uniformed women peacekeepers as the reflection of heavily masculine national-level military and police structures and the under representation of women in these structures. Therefore, the low participation of uniformed women peacekeepers is simply the non-availability of women in the pool from which TCCs/PCCs draw their recruitment for UN deployment (Coomaraswamy,

2015:13). Due to this perception, a great deal of attention has been diverted to the UN on the need for a National Action Plan in the TCCs/PCCs to increase the recruitment and retention of women in the national security sector.

Some have mixed up peacekeepers as mercenaries and suggested that TCCs/PCCs be incentivised by offering monetary incentives to provide more women peacekeepers for the UN mission (Kenny, 2016; Bigio, and Vogelstein, 2018).

Even the developed countries, which have achieved greater gender parity in their military and police sectors, have not contributed the required number of uniformed women peacekeepers for UN operations (Coomaraswamy, 2015:139). So, it is not only the low contribution by the developing countries that prevented the UN from achieving the numerical target of increasing the uniformed women peacekeepers.

Challenges of Uniformed Women's Participation

Although great importance has been accorded to the participation of uniformed women peacekeepers, the uniformed women peacekeepers confront a series of challenges in the operational field. One of the most glaring challenges is that instead of accepting gender mainstreaming as the responsibility of whole-of-mission, the gendered division of labour and role segregation has been practiced in the operational field. The male peacekeepers seem to have a superficial understanding of gender and they perceive gender mainstreaming as the responsibility of women peacekeepers.

Further, the uniformed women peacekeepers' specific traits such as compassion, soft posture, and unique skill in engagement with the local community are highlighted at the cost of their professionalism and other skills as military or police personnel. It restricts uniformed women peacekeepers' potential and under-utilises their skills and capabilities. This mind-set among the UN leaders reinforces the traditional stereotype notions of women and they tend to conflate uniformed women peacekeepers with local women who need protection and keep them at the base, instead of doing active duties like their male colleagues (Baldwin and Taylor, 2020: 1).

The uniformed women peacekeepers are also confronted with the challenge of high expectations of them to promote the effectiveness of the mission. It creates additional burdens for the uniformed women peacekeepers and they are obliged to undertake volunteer tasks in the form of a second shift to prove their worthiness. The uniformed women are invariably involved in outreach programmes in the local community, spending their immense energy and personal time to carry out these outreach programmes. The second shift role of the uniformed women peacekeepers emerged not because of natural traits or instincts of women but social expectations for women peacekeepers. This expectation actually perpetuates gendered differences, requiring the uniformed women peacekeepers to do extra unpaid work in the UN mission (Pruitt, 2016: 73). It makes the uniformed women peacekeepers feel that they have additional reasonability for the success of UN peacekeeping efforts and sustaining peace.

The uniformed women peacekeepers faced the challenge of additional scrutiny during deployment as they are perceived to be "incapable, vulnerable, and weak." This perception in the UN peacekeeping operations has arisen because the uniformed women peacekeepers are considered a "woman first, soldier second" (Vermeij, 2020:13).

The uniformed women peacekeepers themselves are confronted with the challenge of harassment and abuse within the missions. Some authors have highlighted discriminatory behaviour and sexism the uniformed women peacekeepers confronted. Because of the male peacekeepers' lack of trust and acceptance, the uniformed women peacekeepers are given unequal tasks, limiting the opportunities to utilise their professional skills and capabilities (Vermeij, 2020:14; Baldwin and Taylor 2020). Because of the discriminatory treatment, the UN Security Council had to adopt a resolution in 2020 urging to "strengthen their collective efforts to promote the full, effective, and meaningful participation of uniformed and civilian women in peacekeeping operations at all levels and in all positions, including in senior leadership positions… (identify and address) barriers in the recruitment, deployment, and promotion of uniformed women peacekeepers" (UNSC, 2020). The resolution also urged "to ensure safe, enabling and gender-sensitive working environments for women in peacekeeping operations and to address threats and violence against them".

The uniformed women peacekeepers also faced the challenges of biases in deployment selection by the authorities in TCCs/PCCs. They also miss the opportunity to serve in the UN missions as they lack awareness of the UN's deployment options for women. Due to these challenges, UN Security Council adopted a resolution urging "to disseminate information about and providing access to deployment opportunities for women personnel, including for senior positions; provide access to training for uniformed women personnel, and ensuring that trained uniformed women are deployed for peacekeeping operations; highlighted the need to develop a national database of trained women personnel interested in and available for nomination and deployment; and need to identify and address barriers in the recruitment, deployment, and promotion of uniformed women peacekeepers" (UNSC, 2020).

The uniformed women peacekeepers are also confronted with the challenge of lack of women-specific equipment and accommodation, inadequate living conditions, and other facilities, which prevent the creation of a conducive working environment and hamper the utilisation of the full potential of the uniformed women peacekeepers. Due to these challenges, UN Security Council "urges the UN Secretariat or TCC/PCCs, where appropriate, to provide adequate and appropriate infrastructure and facilities for women in the missions, such as accommodation, sanitation, health care, protective equipment, taking into account their specific needs as well as demands with regard to security and privacy, further urges the Member States and the UN Secretariat to make available adequate resources in this regard" (UNSC, 2020).

Even the Global Study on the Implementation of UN Security Council Resolution 1325 of 2015 recommended sufficient funds be allocated to better accommodate greater numbers of women among military contingents through necessary changes in mission facilities and life such as "special family or leave arrangements for women, adequate and appropriate mission facilities for women - from accommodation quarters and sanitary facilities to welfare and recreational spaces and activities, special medical and gynaecological care, gender-specific uniforms or body armour; and investments in the internal safety of the compound, among others" (Coomaraswamy, 2015:142).

Usually, the uniformed women peacekeepers are deployed in male-dominated mixed units. They are mostly assigned supportive as opposed to direct impact roles. They are assigned stereotypical jobs such as desk work, medical service, and other supporting tasks. Such co-deployment or mixed units are more likely to be tokenism (Pruitt, 2016: 110).

Most of these challenges have arisen as the UN perceive uniformed women peacekeepers' involvement from an instrumentalist perspective, neglecting the right-based equality and gender empowerment categories of the UN Resolution 1325. Even the high-ranking officials and important UN documents focus on instrumentalist justification. For example, Ex-UN Secretary-General Ban Ki-Moon held such a view as he has said "Gender parity is as important here [in policing] as it is across our agenda. It is not an end in itself. It is a means to an end: greater efficiency, greater effectiveness (Ki-Moon, 2010). Even the report of the High-Level Independent Panel on UN Peace Operations pointed out the instrumentalist perspective of uniformed women peacekeepers' role (United Nations, 2015). The present UN Secretary-General António Guterres also stated at the UN Security Council, "This is not just a question of numbers, but also of our effectiveness in fulfilling our mandates" (Guterres, 2019). Even the UN peacekeeping website which deals with "Why is it important to have women peacekeepers?" has not delved into the right-based gender equality aspect of uniformed women's participation in the UN peace operations (United Nations Peacekeeping, nb).

Resolution 1325 expects gender equality and representativeness to be seen as ends in themselves and the UN peace operations require making gender equality central to all their activities. The rights-based approach to gender equality would have highlighted the need for gender parity as the women have opted for careers in the military and police forces for the same practical reasons as men, such as stable jobs, decent salaries, good benefits, and opportunities to challenge themselves, proof their capability and professionalism even in these male-dominated and masculinised oriented services. The women become peacekeepers "not primarily to help other women, but rather to improve their own career prospects or increase their earning potential" (Jennings, 2013:62). The dominance of the instrumentalist discourse denies the crucial need to challenge embedded stereotypes and undermine the discourse on the problems of inequality. It is ironic that the uniformed women peacekeepers, who are required to promote gender equality in the local community in their areas of deployment, do not have their right to equality emphasised in the UN missions.

The High-Level Panel on Peacekeeping Operations report noted several areas in which UN peacekeeping operations are falling short in implementing the Women, Peace and Security Agenda. It specifically acknowledged that even after fifteen years of the adoption of Resolution 1325, "there remains a poor understanding of the potential of both integrating a gendered perspective and increasing the participation of women at all levels of political and civil life, most especially at the leadership level" (United Nations, 2015).

Instead of making attempt to address these challenges of the uniformed women peacekeepers in the operational field and other important aspects of gender in the conflict areas, the UN seems to be excessively focused on sexual violence committed by the male peacekeepers and international humanitarian workers in the conflict areas. Resolutions, 1829 (2008), 1888 (2009), 1960 (2010), 2106 (2013), 2122 (2013), 2272 (2016), and 2467 (2019) took as their main focus the protection of women and girls from conflict-related sexual violence (CRSV) and sexual exploitation and abuse (SEA). There is no doubt that this problem has sullied the overall reputation of peacekeeping missions and profoundly embarrassed the UN. However, the excessive focus on the perpetrators and not dealing much with how to handle the survivors, and overlooking other major issues undermines the implementation of resolution 1325. The upshot of the predominant focus on CRSV and SEA meant that the mainstreaming of gender in the UN peacekeeping operations accord importance to protection and prevention above equality and gender empowerment mandate of Resolution 1325.

Conclusion

It is definitely an achievement to upgrade women from the development agenda to the peace and security agenda. However, the rhetoric of significance of uniformed women's participation in the UN peacekeeping operation has not matched the conducive facilities and opportunities in the operational field. Women continue to bear the burden of conflict and uniformed women peacekeepers continue to suffer from discriminatory practices and expectations. The instrumentalist approach to uniformed women's role in peacekeeping operations undermines the right to equality and gender empowerment, which are equally important components of resolution 1325. The uniformed women peacekeepers lack the opportunity to fully utilise their professional skills and capabilities in the UN missions. As discussed above, they were confronted with numerous challenges, which could have been resolved through conscious efforts by the UN and member states. Instead, the attention of the UN seems to be diverted to dealing with auxiliary issues such as National Action Plan, CRSV, and SEA. The UN Security Council's sustained attention to rape and sexual violence by the male UN peacekeepers and international humanitarian actors distracts the attention from the core issues. The UN Security Council seems to become conscious of the challenges faced by the uniformed women peacekeepers only in 2020 when it adopted the resolution on 28 August, which for the first time highlighted the series of requirements to make the operational environment conducive for uniformed women's recruitment and participation.

The way forward for effective participation of uniformed women peacekeepers is to make conscious attempts to establish enabling operational environment in the field. There is also a need for suitable training and effective accountability mechanisms to ensure that gender mainstreaming is the responsibility of the whole mission. Above all, gender equality and gender empowerment should be accorded equal importance as gender protection and gender participation, as intended in resolution 1325.

References

Baldwin, Gretchen, and Taylor, Sarah (2020), "Uniformed Women in Peace Operations: Challenging Assumptions and Transforming Approaches," New York: International Peace Institute.

Bigio, Jamille and Vogelstein, Rachel B. (2018), "Increasing Female Participation in Peacekeeping Operations," New York: Council on Foreign Relations.

Coomaraswamy, Radhika (2015), *Preventing Conflict, Transforming Justice, Securing the Peace: A Global Study on the Implementation of United Nations Security Council Resolution 1325*, UN Women.

Department of Peacekeeping Operations and Department of Field Support (DPKO/DFS) (2010), "Guidelines Integrating a Gender Perspective into the Work of The United Nations Military in Peacekeeping Operations," New York: Department of Peacekeeping Operations and Department of Field Support.

Department of Peace Operations (2018), *Uniformed Gender Parity Strategy 2018-2028*, New York: Department of Peace Operations.

Ferrari, Sofia Sacks (2019), "Is the United Nations Uniformed Gender Parity Strategy on track to reach its goals?" Solna: Stockholm International Peace Research Institute (SIPRI).

Guterres, António (2019), "Deployment of Female Personnel Boosts Effectiveness, Says Secretary-General, as Security Council Holds Open Debate on Women in Peacekeeping," 8508th Meeting, SC/13773, 11 April, available at https://www.un.org/press/en/2019/sc13773.doc.htm, accessed on 23 January 2022.

Holt, Victoria and Taylor, Glyn with Max Kelly (2009), *Protecting Civilians in the Context of UN Peacekeeping Operations: Success, Setbacks and Remaining Challenges*, New York: Department of Peacekeeping Operations and the Office of the Coordination of Humanitarian Affairs.

Jennings, Kathleen M (2011), 'Women's participation in UN peacekeeping operations: agents of change or stranded symbols?' Norwegian Peacebuilding Resource Centre (NOREF).

Karim, Sabrina and Beardsley, Kyle (2013), 'Female Peacekeepers and Gender Balancing: Token Gestures or Informed Policymaking?' *International Interactions*, vol. 39, issue 4, pp. 461-488.

Kenny, Charles (2016), "Using Financial Incentives to Increase the Number of Women in UN Peacekeeping," Washington D.C.: Centre for Global Development.

Kreft, Anne-Kathrin (2017), "The gender mainstreaming gap: Security Council resolution 1325 and UN peacekeeping mandates," *International Peacekeeping*, Vol. 24, No. 1, pp. 132-158.

Pruitt, Lesley J. (2016), *The women in blue helmets: gender, policing, and the UN's first all-female peacekeeping unit*, Oakland: University of California Press.

Tidblad-Lundholm, Kajsa (2020), "When are Women Deployed? Operational Uncertainty and Deployment of Female Personnel to UN Peacekeeping," *International Peacekeeping*, Vol. 27, No. 4, pp. 673-702.

United Nations (2015), "Uniting our Strengths for Peace – Politics, Partnership and People, Report of the High-Level

Independent Panel on Peace Operations (HIPPO)", New York: United Nations Publication Office.

United Nations Peacekeeping (na), "Promoting Women, Peace and Security," https://peacekeeping.un.org/en/promoting-women-peace-and-security

United Nations Peacekeeping (nb), "Women in Peacekeeping", available at https://peacekeeping.un.org/en/women-peacekeeping, accessed on 25 February 2022.

United Nations Peacekeeping (nc), 'Gender Statistic-August 2006,' available at https://peacekeeping.un.org/sites/default/files/aug06.pdf, accessed on 3 February 2022.

United Nations Peacekeeping (nd), 'Gender,' available at https://peacekeeping.un.org/sites/default/files/summary_of_troop_contributions_to_un_peacekeeping_operations_by_mission_post_and_gender.pdf, accessed on 22 February 2022.

United Nations Security Council (UNSC) (2000), S/RES/1325 (2000), 31 October.

United Nations Security Council (UNSC) (2015), S/RES/2242 (2015) 13 October.

United Nations Security Council (UNSC) (2020), S/RES/2538 (2020), 28 August.

UN Women (n), 'The United Nations Fourth World Conference on Women: Platform for Action,' available at https://www.un.org/womenwatch/daw/beijing/platform/armed.htm, accessed on 24 February 2022

Vermeij, Lotte (2020), "Woman First, Soldier Second: Taboos and Stigmas Facing Military Women in UN Peace Operations," October, New York: International Peace Institute.

An overview of the Women, Peace and Security and challenges – the perspective of an academician

Dr Tasneem Meenai

Introduction

The post-Cold War period has witnessed an increasing number of intra-state conflicts characterised by high levels of violence targeting civilians and greatly undermining the human rights of vulnerable populations, especially women and children. Women and girls faced particular difficulties both during armed conflict as well as in the aftermath of violent conflicts. In the backdrop of these violent intra-state conflicts, several initiatives were undertaken at the United Nations (UN) to ensure the protection of these vulnerable populations.

The post-cold war years were also characterised by immense changes in UN peacekeeping and peacebuilding operations, as the UN became more engaged in intra-state conflicts. The adoption of UN Security Council Resolution (UNSCR) 1325 on 31 October 2000 brought renewed focus on Women, Peace, and Security (WPS) at the UN. Known widely as the **WPS agenda,** the resolution "reaffirms the important role of women in the prevention and resolution of conflicts, peace negotiations, peacebuilding, peacekeeping, humanitarian response and in post-conflict reconstruction and stresses the importance of their equal participation and full involvement in all efforts for the maintenance and promotion of peace and security."[1]

A range of issues pertaining to the protection of women and girls during and after the violent conflict were identified and needed to be addressed urgently. It was also observed that women were particularly under-represented in the peace processes that followed violent conflicts thereby minimising the chances of creating sustainable peace. In UNSCR 1325, the Security Council laid stress on the crucial role that women can play in promoting the gender dimension in UNs' efforts in maintaining international peace and security.

This article provides an overview of the Women, Peace, and Security agenda and its challenges. The paper is presented in two sections. The first section will provide the institutional and policy guidelines of the WPS agenda at the UN and look into the existing approaches to promote WPS in UN Peace Operations. The second section will focus on implementing of the WPS agenda in UN Peace Operations in the context of conflict-related sexual violence (CRSV) and the challenges confronted therein.

Section - I Women, Peace, and Security and UN Peace Operations

UN peace operations in the post cold war period consisted of narrowly focused military responses with scant attention paid to addressing the particular needs of women affected by conflict and violence. "Women were overlooked from peacekeeping operations and were also excluded from subsequent peace processes."[2]

---

1   https://www.un.org/womenwatch/osagi/wps/ accessed on 07 February, 2022.

2   Global Handbook on Parliaments as Partners Supporting the Women, Peace and Security Agenda implemented by the United Nations Development Programme (UNDP), 2019, p. 6. https://www.

Issues of incorporating the gender perspective in UN peace operations and of gender mainstreaming were first brought on its agenda by the Special Committee on Peacekeeping Operations in 1999. The high-level Panel convened by the Secretary-General in 2000 conducted a review of UN peace and security activities which brought out the Report of the Panel on UN Peace Operations. One of the important highlights of the report was to recognise the need for equitable gender representation in the leadership of peacekeeping missions. The Windhoek Declaration and the Namibia Plan of Action on Mainstreaming a Gender Perspective in Multi-dimensional Peace Support Operations (S/2000/693) was a critical step in the adoption of UNSCR 1325 which also recognised the need for specialised training for all peacekeeping personnel on the protection, special needs and human rights of women and children in conflict situations.[3]

With respect to protection issues and prevention of violence against women, as mentioned in UNSCR 1325, "the gender perspectives in each of the activities undertaken in the framework of protection needs to be explicitly identified and addressed. For example, protection from, and prevention of, violence including gender-based and sexual violence, necessitates monitoring and reporting all forms of violence against women and girls, and setting up mechanisms for addressing needs created by violence, including counseling, legal, medical, and other forms of material support."[4]

---

undp.org/content/dam/undp/library/peace/conflict-prevention-peacebuilding/Parliament_as_partners_supporting_the_Women_Peace_and_Security_Agenda_-_A_Global_Handbook.pdf , accessed on 31.01.2022.

3 Women, Peace and Security Study submitted by the Secretary-General pursuant to Security Council resolution 1325 (2000) 2002, p.109 https://www.un.org/womenwatch/daw/public/eWPS.pdf, accessed on 07.02.2022.

4 Ibid. p. 109.

These concerns were subsequently addressed when nine more UNSC Resolutions were adopted to strengthen the WPS agenda and its implementation by further identifying specific areas where women's equal participation and full involvement were needed to promote peace and security. The WPS agenda developed into a "full-fledged policy and institutional framework" with four central pillars of engagement for women in conflict settings: prevention, participation, protection, and relief and recovery. These four pillars of WPS can be understood as:

1. Prevention - Prevention of conflict and all forms of violence against women and girls in conflict and post-conflict situations.

2. Participation - Women's equal participation and gender equality in peace and security decision-making processes at all levels.

3. Protection - Women and girls are protected from all forms of sexual and gender-based violence and their rights are protected and promoted in conflict situations and

4. Relief and Recovery - Specific relief needs of women are met and their capacities to act as agents in and recovery are strengthened in conflict and post-conflict situations.[5]

Of the ten resolutions adopted, two deal with agenda setting [1325 (2000) and 2242 (2015)], three resolutions deal with participation [1889 (2010), 2122 (2013) and 2493 (2019)], and five resolutions focus on protection of women [1820 (2009), 1888 (2009), 1960 (2011), 2106 (2013), and 2467 (2019)], in particular from sexual violence.[6]

---

5   Global Handbook on Parliaments as Partners, p. 5.

6   OECD, Twentieth Anniversary of UN Security Council Resolution

These ten WPS - centred UN resolutions have focused on several peace functions "stressing the importance of women's leadership and meaningful participation in the prevention and resolution of conflicts; addressing the impact of sexual violence; promoting the development and use of measures and standards for monitoring the implementation of women, peace and security mandates; training and capacity building on gender equality and women, peace and security for peacekeeping personnel; engaging with civil society more comprehensively and enabling an improved understanding of gender dynamics of conflict."[7]

It has been observed that women were generally invisible in conflict analysis as victims, survivors, peace-builders, and perpetrators of violence. The gender perspective in international relations and peace and conflict studies has brought the focus on and recognition of women's agency and the immense potential they have in contributing to peace. The WPS agenda is considered as having "significant potential to bring knowledge and social transformation to prevent conflicts, protect human rights, and promote recovery from conflict and insecurity."[8]

The promotion and effective implementation of the WPS agenda in UN peace operations is tested on the basis of the delivery of WPS-specific mandates given by the UN Security Council in the context of contemporary armed

---

1325: Financing gender equality and women's empowerment in fragile contexts https://www.oecd.org/development/gender-development/OECD-Gendernet-Financing-UNSCR.pdf accessed on 31.01.2022.

7   Promoting Women, Peace and Security https://peacekeeping.un.org/en/promoting-women-peace-and-security

8   Sara E. Davies and Jacqui True, Women, Peace and Security – A Transformative Agenda? In Sara E. Davies and Jacqui True Eds. The Oxford Handbook of Women, Peace and Security, 2019, p. 3.

conflicts. The complex and multi-dimensional nature of UN peacekeeping and peacebuilding operations is the result of the continuous and evolving engagement of the UN through its conflict prevention, peacekeeping, peacemaking, and peacebuilding activities in armed conflicts especially in the post-cold war period. It has been contended that "peace and security can only be achieved and sustained if all members of society are equal in terms of opportunities, protection, access to resources and services and participation in decision making".[9]

This reflects the liberal, humanitarian, developmental, and democratic conception of peace which broadly forms the basis on which UN Peace Operations have been undertaken.

Consequently, the WPS agenda also finds its expression through the liberal, humanitarian, developmental, and democratic approaches adopted in UN peace operations. The liberal approach is meant to promote women's freedoms and gender equality in peacekeeping and peacebuilding interventions, the humanitarian approach is meant to protect women from all kinds of violence within the framework of International Humanitarian Law, International Human Rights Law, International Criminal Law, and International Refugee Law. The purpose of the developmental approach is to enable the participation of women in development activities through access to resources and opportunities based on women empowerment and equity in post-conflict recovery and reconstruction. The democratic approach is meant to remove any discrimination on the basis of gender and for providing equal opportunities to women for political participation in order to broad base the process of democratic participation and decision-making in post-conflict societies.

---

9   Women Peace and Security (WPS) in Peacekeeping Operations, https://peacekeeping.un.org/sites/default/files/dpo_key_message_english.pdf, accessed on 31.01.2022.

Section - II   UN Peace Operations and protection of women from conflict-related sexual violence (CRSV)

It is now universally acknowledged that the WPS agenda is "a significant international normative and policy framework addressing the gender-specific impacts of conflict on women and girls."[10] Since the adoption of UNSCR 1325 in 2000, UN peace operations have made some progress in advancing the agenda on women, peace, and security. Women have become increasingly involved in prevention and mediation efforts led by UN special envoys and in the integration of gender dimensions into policies and strategies for electoral assistance and protection of civilians. Increased training and capacity building on gender equality and women, peace, and security for peacekeeping personnel is being undertaken. Also, women are involved with civil society organisations in a more comprehensive manner and are contributing towards an improved understanding of gender dynamics of conflict as well as in the promotion of gender mainstreaming across all mandated tasks.[11]

Yet, over the last two decades, it has also been observed that women and girls continue to bear the burden of armed conflict where "structural power inequalities that contribute to Sexual and Gender-Based Violence (SGBV) greatly deepen and are manifested in various forms including as Conflict-Related Sexual Violence (CRSV)."[12] UNSCR 1820 (2008)

10　Davies and True, Op. cit.

11　Preventing Conflict Transforming Justice Securing the Peace - A Global Study on the Implementation of United Nations Security Council Resolution 1325, UN Women, 2015, p. 80. https://wps. unwomen.org/pdf/en/GlobalStudy_EN_Web.pdf　accessed　on 07.02.2022.

12　https://peacekeeping.un.org/sites/default/files/dpo_pages_ participation_protection_prevention_sgbv_combined.pdf recognises sexual violence as a tactic of war and a matter of international peace and security that necessitates a security response.[13]

According to the Department of Peace Operation, "Conflict-Related Sexual Violence refers to rape, sexual slavery, forced prostitution, forced pregnancy, forced abortion, enforced sterilisation, forced marriage, trafficking in persons when committed in situations of conflict for the purpose of sexual violence/exploitation and any other form of sexual violence of comparable gravity perpetrated against women, men, girls or boys that is directly or indirectly linked to a conflict."[14] Armed forces of parties to a conflict are considered as the main perpetrators of CRSV on the basis of evidence from several conflicts which indicates that members of fighting forces have specifically targeted women and adolescent girls. [15]Although peacekeeping troops have been associated with sexual exploitation and abuse, the vast majority of peacekeepers carry out their duties with professionalism.[16]

The WPS agenda addresses the issue of CRSV through several provisions. Resolution 1325 calls on all parties to armed conflict to take special measures to protect women and girls from gender-based violence, particularly rape

---

13 Department of Peace Operations, Gender Equality and Women, Peace and Security Resource Package, New York, 2020, p. 13. https://peacekeeping.un.org/sites/default/files/gewps19_respack_v7_eng_digital_4.pdf accessed on 01.02.2022.

14 Ibid. p. 9.

15 Women, Peace and Security Study, p. 28, https://www.un.org/womenwatch/daw/public/eWPS.pdf accessed on 07.02.2022.

16 Elisabeth Rehn and Ellen Johnson Sirleaf, Women War Peace – The Independent Experts' Assessment on the Impact of Armed Conflict on Women and Women's Role in Peace-building, UNIFEM, 2002 p. 71.

and other forms of sexual abuse, and all other forms of violence in situations of armed conflict. Resolution 1820 requests the Secretary-General and relevant UN agencies, to develop effective mechanisms for providing protection from violence, including in particular sexual violence, to women and girls in and around UN-managed refugee and Internally Displaced Person (IDP) camps. Resolution 1888 calls on all parties to armed conflict to immediately take appropriate measures to protect civilians, including women and children, from all forms of sexual violence. It also calls for establishing a Special Representative of the Secretary-General and a team of experts on the rule of law and improving coordination among stakeholders on sexual violence in conflict. Resolution 1960 "calls upon parties to armed conflict to make and implement specific and time-bound commitments to combat sexual violence, which should include, inter alia, issuance of clear orders through chains of command prohibiting sexual violence and the prohibition of sexual violence in Codes of Conduct, military field manuals, or equivalent; and further calls upon those parties to make and implement specific commitments on the timely investigation of alleged abuses in order to hold perpetrators accountable."[17]

UNSCR 1325, 1820, and 2467 call upon peacekeeping operations to act to combat SGBV, particularly against women and children, and to prosecute perpetrators. By addressing structural gender norms and expectations that fuel conflict and insecurity, peacekeeping missions contribute to preventing, mitigating, and responding to SGBV.[18] In 2007, the Secretary-General formed UN Action against Sexual Violence in Conflict, a coordinating body that unites the work of 13 UN entities working to end

---

17   A Global Study on the Implementation of UNSCR 1325, pp. 66-67.

18   https://peacekeeping.un.org/sites/default/files/dpo_pages_
participation_protection_prevention_sgbv_combined.pdf

sexual violence in conflict, and in 2009 the Security Council requested the appointment of the Special Representative on Sexual Violence in Conflict."[19]

As mentioned above, UNSCR 1325 highlights the gendered aspects of war and armed conflict demanding the protection of women's rights, including shielding women and girls from gender-based violence and other violations of international law, and also urged all parties to conflict to take special measures to protect women and girls from gender-based violence, particularly rape and other forms of sexual abuse, in situations of armed conflict.[20] The Global Study on the Implementation of UNSCR 1325, published by the UN Secretary-General in 2015, "revealed that while the women, peace and security agenda had contributed to significant changes in international norms surrounding women's political leadership and decision-making on peace and security, its effect on the lives of women at local levels has been limited." [21]

Amongst the many structural, institutional, and socio-cultural factors that pose challenges to implementing WPS, "patriarchy, inequalities, militarised masculinities, and discriminatory power structures inhibit effective conflict prevention, inclusive peace, women's rights, and participation."[22] Women, therefore, remain marginalised in peace processes and in peacebuilding efforts. The protection of women from Conflict-Related Sexual Violence (CRSV) and Sexual Exploitation and Abuse (SEA) constitutes serious

---

19 Global Study on the Implementation of UNSCR 1325, p. 31.

20 Landmark Resolution on Women, Peace, and Security, https://www.un.org/womenwatch/osagi/wps/   accessed on 03.02.2022.

21 A Global Study on the Implementation of UNSCR 1325, p. 4.

22 Why Women, Peace and Security, http://www.peacewomen.org/why-WPS , accessed on 30.01.2022

challenges that render women most vulnerable both during armed conflict and in its aftermath. Moreover, the UN has also received significant criticism for failing to stop cases of Sexual Exploitation and Abuse (SEA) perpetrated by UN peacekeepers, and the culture of impunity for these crimes.

CRSV cases have been documented in Angola, Bosnia and Herzegovina, Cambodia, East Timor, Kosovo, Liberia, Mozambique, and Sierra Leone. Currently, UN Field Missions with a conflict-related sexual violence mandate are operating in Somalia (United Nations Assistance Mission in Somalia), Central African Republic (United Nations Multidimensional Integrated Stabilization Mission in The Central African Republic), Mali (United Nations Multidimensional Integrated Stabilization Mission in Mali), the Democratic Republic of Congo (The United Nations Organization Stabilization Mission in the Democratic Republic of the Congo), Iraq (United Nations Assistance Mission for Iraq), Darfur (African Union-United Nations Hybrid Operation in Darfur) and South Sudan (United Nations Mission in South Sudan).[23]

To remedy the challenges arising from CRSV and SEA it has been recommended that women's presence may be increased in UN peace operations. This has been based on normative and functionalist arguments. The normative argument is that the UN must promote gender equality through its actions by improving the "representativeness and diversity" of its personnel in peace operations. The functionalist argument professes that an increased presence

---

23 The Handbook of UN Field Missions on Prevention and Responding to Conflict-Related Sexual Violence, UN, 2020, p. 3. https://www.un.org/ sexualviolenceinconflict/wp-content/ uploads/2020/06/2020.08-UN-CRSV-Handbook.pdf accessed on 04.02.2022.

of women in UN peace operations improves operational effectiveness.

UN peace operations have made some progress in advancing the WPS agenda to promote peace and security through concerted action by the UN and member states, non-governmental organisations, regional organisations, civil society, and other stakeholders. Many States have also volunteered to hold themselves to account for obligations contained in the WPS agenda. As of September 2021, 98 countries have adopted National Action Plans (NAPs) for the implementation of resolution 1325—policy documents to domesticate its obligations on women's engagement in peace and security and the protection of women in conflict.[24] Another significant development has been the deployment of women protection advisors alongside gender advisors in peace operations and the establishment of an Informal Experts Group on Women, Peace, and Security meant to routinely brief the UNSC on peace operations as per provisions in UNSCR 1960 (2009) and 2242 (2019) respectively.

Despite these positive developments, there remains a deficit in the understanding of the potential of both integrating a gendered perspective and of increasing the participation of women at all levels of political and civil life. The *Global Study on the Implementation of Resolution 1325* (2015) noted that "much of the progress towards the implementation of UNSCR 1325 continues to be measured in "firsts", rather than as standard practice. Obstacles and challenges still persist and prevent the full implementation of the WPS agenda."[25]

---

24 Global Study on the Implementation of UNSCR 1325, p. 32.

25 ibid. p. 14.

Conclusion

The renewed focus on WPS was brought by the Secretary General's Action for Peacekeeping (A4P) initiative, launched in March 2018, which reaffirms that women's full, equal and meaningful participation in peace processes and political solutions is essential for effective peacekeeping. The implementation of WPS priorities is a political commitment in the Action for Peacekeeping Initiative which has currently received 150 endorsements from member states, which also includes endorsements from four regional organisations, who have together expressed support and have committed themselves to the initiative. The A4P initiative is expected to pave the way for the strengthening of the WPS agenda in UN peace operations in the future.

Peculiar challenges to protecting women in the conflict zone – experiences of a peacekeeper from the field

Lt Col Vanessa Hanarahan

The subject of Women's Peace and Security is very important and has seen much improvement and development in recent years. I had the opportunity to serve as a female police member deployed in support of both the United Nations (UN) and NATO.

It has been my experience that the UN and all contributing nations supporting UN missions have improved in addressing the role of women in peace and security, from the perspective of both the integration of female peacekeepers and that of addressing the Protection of Civilians (PoC), specifically vulnerable populations. But there is most certainly more work to be done and this is where I will focus my commentary. The first aspect that I would like to address is what I consider to be aspects that UN peacekeepers, both male and female do to improve the protection of women in conflict zones.

Based on my experiences during both UN and NATO operations, one action that a peacekeeper can do is to enhance the role of local/host nation women at the tactical level. That is to say that peacekeepers need to ensure that the integration of women is better carried out during peacekeeper engagements in local communities and villages. For example, on all missions, there are key leadership engagements (KLEs) that take place with the senior representatives of every village or community. What I have noted during my experiences is that the female members of the community are not often in attendance and if they are, it is with the permission of the male elders. Further, females do not actually engage in the discussion nor do peacekeepers attempt to engage them in the discussions. Being aware of this a peacekeeper can proactively engage the female members of the community to solicit their involvement and integration at all KLEs. When noting that there is no female representation, the peacekeeper can request or encourage the village elders to include female members at the start of the KLE. Actions such as this reinforce the importance and value that the UN places on the inclusion of women in the peace process.

Yet another way to enhance the inclusion of female representation is to improve peacekeeper awareness. That is to say that all persons have biases, both conscious and unconscious, and to be aware of this permits one to diminish the effects of these biases on how one functions during peace operations. This point speaks directly to my previous comment about community engagement. We as peacekeepers may deploy on a mission with our ideas regarding the role of women, some may be in line with that of the UN and some may not. Persons must be aware of this and work to ensure that they are adopting the perspectives of the UN and encouraging all women to be more empowered within the domain of peace and security. A heightened sense of personal awareness will permit a peacekeeper to be more cognizant of their need to acknowledge the important role that females play within the peace and security framework.

Further, the placement of UN female peacekeepers in senior or strategic positions will reinforce and provide an example for the local population to emulate. For me, the lead by example approach is always most effective. In my opinion seeing female peacekeepers leading a KLE, leading the UN peacekeeper team in a village, or being placed in command positions must happen. Being the face of the UN to the local population reinforces that female is not only capable but is an essential part of the conversation when addressing peace and security. Females should be seen as having an equal voice. Encouraging the local community to take an integrated and inclusive approach to peace and security is the next step and a necessary one if there is to be recognition of the importance of women in the safety and stability of a country or region. Women too are to be seen as a powerful and empowering image in the community. To apply this concept to real life I will highlight that as the Force Provost Marshal for UNMISS I was the only female within the mission of 15000 military members at the rank of Colonel or above. For me, it is not only about an increase in the total number of females within peace operations, but it is about meaningful participation. This must include the presence of females within leadership and key positions, positions where females can effect change and influence operations. We must ensure there are no systemic processes or internal biases within our militaries that impede the ability of females to have equal opportunity within the UN structure.

A female presence in the UN demonstrates the capabilities of females. Female police and military members act as a means of inspiring host nation females to speak up and become involved. It gives them confidence that they are important and can contribute to the peace and security of their country. Empowering women is an efficient means of improving their willingness to face the dangers and improve their quality of life and that of their children. It has been my experience on every mission when engaging with the local female population I have been humbled by their comments about how seeing a woman in uniform, and integrated with their male counterparts inspires them to change the situation for themselves and their daughters. In Afghanistan for example I was told that seeing women in a uniform inspired Afghan females to join the Afghan police. The sheer presence of a female peacekeeper can have a profound impact on the aspiring younger generation to become involved, speak up, and make a difference.

At the operational and strategic level diversity is a strength. That is to say that female military and police persons provide varying perspectives to the planning process of UN missions at all levels. When developing a mission operational plan females in the room ensure that there is a more holistic approach to the reduction of violence against women. Who better than a female to assist in determining how one should face problems affecting women? As a result of this diversity, the initial plans created are better developed to face all potential situations.

Finally, female military and police members' presence provides a platform for some females to come forward and talk about the violence that they are experiencing. It has been proven that most females are more comfortable speaking with other females when discussing sensitive matters, specifically violence that they face every day. Again, the use of female engagement teams in UNMISS is an excellent example of how the presence of females has improved the interactions between the local female population and the UN, thereby allowing the UN to know and react to the violence. Knowledge is power. Knowing that violence is taking place in a community or village ensures that one can then find a means to address the problem. Without the female military and police persons, the UN would not be privy to the same level of information, meaning that they would be less effective at curbing the existence of violence. With a better understanding of the intelligence picture, the UN can better develop plans that accurately address the violence of women and other vulnerable populations. Knowing that violence against women is taking place is essential to finding a way to eliminate or at least diminish the level of violence taking place.

In conclusion, as previously noted, the women, peace, and security program of the UN has achieved much greatness and the level of integration within the UN has improved over the past decade. The presence of women within all levels of the UN System as well as better female integration at the tactical level must continue to grow. It is through awareness, presence, and perseverance that success will be achieved. Through better integration of women within all military and police forces around the world, contributing nations of the UN will be better poised to support the UN as it endeavours to empower women across the globe to rise up and participate in peace and security.

Special Remarks by Women Peacekeepers

Commandant Poonam Gupta

India fulfilled commitment it made in September 2006, to assist the UN Peacekeeping operations in Liberia by sending the first All women Formed Police Unit (FPU) to Liberia (UNMIL) on 30 January 2007. This marked another first in the history of UN Peacekeeping, an All-female contingent joined peacekeeping operations to strengthen the rule of law & maintain peace. The main activities undertaken by the FPU were:

a) Training of Liberian National Police (LNP).

b) Provided medical cover to nearby communities.

c) Imparted self-defence skills to Liberian women and girls.

d) Conducted workshops on the prevention of sexual violence.

e) Supported orphanages and schools in line with community engagement.

f) Supported/Mentored Liberian women for joining LNP.

Protecting women in the conflict zone presents several challenges. Some of the common challenges are:

a) In large-scale gender-based violence, sexual violence remains comparatively invisible, statistically underestimated because of cultural constraints and a strong feeling of shame and fear engendered by sexual violence, most victims do not seek help. This adds to the devastating effects on them, their families, and their communities. Victims' inability to get access to economic support and adequate legal remedies. Large-scale displacement leaves women vulnerable to reproductive health, availability of medicine, doctors, and hospitals in refugee camps is a challenge.

b) Displacement during conflicts places women in a vulnerable position to certain kinds of violence. Availability of weapons, and fear of life, limb, and family, threaten women and girls disproportionally highly.

c) Destruction of hospitals, roads, electricity, public transport, and Government facility is a hindrance to protecting women. Conflicts discourage children from attending colleges/schools, leaving generations illiterate. It is also a limiting factor for income generation that leads to poverty and susceptibility to violence & sexual abuse. Conflicts force women to the margins of the administration.

d) Inadequate resources, insufficient training, and unavailable infrastructure are impediments to the effective availability of the criminal justice system. The limited number of blue helmets on the ground leaves many vulnerable areas unattended. Similarly, the UN agencies cannot reach all the affected persons in conflict areas thus many are left inadequately covered.

Despite the challenges, there was some visible impact of the female FPU in Liberia. The participation of women law enforcement agencies in Liberia increased from 7 % to 17% during the deployment of IFPU. There was a fourfold increase in the number of women applying to become Police officers. Ban Ki-Moon, the then UN Secretary-General, referred performance of the All-female IFPU in Liberia, 2016 - "Unwavering performance, professionalism and discipline" and "They managed criminality, deterred sexual and gender-based violence" A few recommendations to enhance the effectiveness of FPU operations are:

a) Provide a secure environment to the victims so that they can come forward with their experiences. Provide treatment, counselling, and legal support for the victims to hold the perpetrators accountable for their actions. Provide educational opportunities to those who have missed education due to violence in form of abridged courses. Build infrastructure for education and eradicate illiteracy.

b) Encourage the Government /communities to increase participation of women. But intake of women in policy-making /higher decision-making bodies will be crucial for greater inclusiveness and gender equality. Empower women to vote, run for office, and to join the Police and the other rule of law institutions to provide support to other women.

c) Establishing Police and other law enforcement agencies and training them to observe international standards of human rights, Policing, and law enforcement. Do away with gender bias, so that people feel comfortable asking for Police help. The community engagement should be long-term. The crimes against women should be effectively dealt with to break the chain of violence. Impartial and fair disputes resolution including land disputes arising out of displacement of the population due to violence.

d) Skill development, employment generation, to save women from falling into trap of violence and sexual abuse. Increase access to social services & health care. Include Police and Military peacekeepers in community outreach.

Special Remarks by Women Peacekeepers

Ms Sangya Malla

Women peacekeepers have been playing a crucial role in the missions as it has been seen that in any conflict situation women and children are mostly affected. Interacting with the vulnerable communities is not an easy task but with my experience in the mission that I am currently serving, MONUSCO, and past experience; I have seen that seeing a woman in field encourages these women to come out of their shells and try to speak out and engage in activities or training. The Police Division has several other initiatives in place to ensure that women are motivated, and inspired. But above all, they are able to meaningfully participate across the full spectrum of police functions, especially in senior leadership positions.

In support of the UN goal of 50/50 gender parity, the Police Division (PD) has sought to identify, mentor, train, and prepare a women-only United Nations Police (UNPOL) Command Cadre composed of nominated senior-ranking policewomen who fulfil all of the requirements for leadership positions as Heads and Deputy Heads of Police Components as well as strategic middle management posts. In August 2021, in collaboration with the Department of Peace Operations and Department of Political and Peacebuilding Affairs, PD supported the launch of a cross-component survey, piloted in MONUSCO, with a view to establishing a mechanism to gather and comparatively analysing the experiences of both uniformed men and women during deployment to UN peace operations. The main objective is to identify barriers that uniquely affect uniformed women. This survey has revealed that more women than men are keen to redeploy. This notwithstanding, more needs to be done to ensure the work culture fosters respect for women and the physical infrastructure is more gender-responsive. These results show that even despite the good efforts of PD and the entire UN, women police officers still face discrimination in peacekeeping. Regrettably, some women are unaware that what they are experiencing is discriminatory behaviour. Member states must request troop-contributing countries to train women and encourage women to join the force so equal participation of females in Peacekeeping is possible and the targeted outcome can be achieved.

More Women in UN Peace Operations: An Agenda for the New Peace Operations

Col (Dr) KK Sharma[1]

Introduction

UN Peace Operations (UNPOs) assist countries to transit from an ongoing conflict to peaceful existence and future prosperity. Peacekeeping has been defined as a cornerstone of peace and security efforts by the UN and its agencies. Since 2000, a new realization had dawned, that women peacekeepers can be a key to UNPO success. UN Security Council resolution 1325 on "Women, Peace and Security", called for the 'full realization of the rights of women to sit at the political table and as the protectors of peace in their own countries'. When compared to 2000 or even 2010, more women are serving the UN as a part of UN military, staff, UN Civilian Police (UNPOL) and other non-uniformed staff or peacekeepers.

On 20 September 2017 an event was held in New York on Gender and Peacekeeping, where progress of the implementation of the women, peace and security (WPS) mandate was reviewed. It called member states for increase in women's deployments in the UNPOs. In 1993, only 1%

---

1   Former Dean and Professor, Chitkara University, ICFAI, and current Research Fellow, USI of India.

of deployed uniformed personnel were women. In 2020, out of approximately 95,000 peacekeepers, women constituted 4.8% of military contingents, 10.9% of UNPOL and 34% of justice and corrections personnel in the UNPO missions. The UN had set a target of 15% women as military observers and staff officers by the end of 2020 and 20% female police deployments. Sadly, the targets were not reached even by the end of 2021. Jean-Pierre Lacroix, current Under-Secretary-General for Peace Operations had lamented that "The number of women deployed in peacekeeping remains too low. We still have a long way to go to achieve parity and implement the women, peace, and security mandates,".

Women have continued to perform a variety of civilian roles in UNPOs since 1948. Most of these roles were in humanitarian, human rights, child protection, development or medical fields. Increasingly, leadership at the UN HQ and field missions have realized that there is no function that can exclude women peacekeepers. They have been deployed to carry out detailed functions in almost all wings of any peace operation both in uniformed or non-uniformed roles. The New York resolution of 20 September 2017 called for a wider role of women in UNPOs, in all functions, military, police, civilians and operational leadership. With protection of civilians, child protection and WPS attaining the focal issue of UNPOs, women peacekeepers have an increased role in protecting civilians, facilitating political processes, promoting human rights, which are the critical components of a mission's success. Many researchers have claimed that deployment of more women invariably helps overall peacekeeping performance in a mission area. They are always better placed to interview and support women and girls, who are the main victims of any conflict. These victims go through gender-based violence. Women peacekeepers mostly act as role models by inspiring local women and girls in male-dominated societies to rise up and be independent.

Global Agenda

Department of UNPO has been working with troop and police-contributing countries (T/PCCs) to increase the number of women in line with the UN Secretary-General's Action for Peacekeeping initiative. The Department had set specific goals for ten years (2018 to 2028) as regards to the percentage share of women peacekeepers in various UN missions. Figure gives out the stated goals for different categories of the peacekeepers.

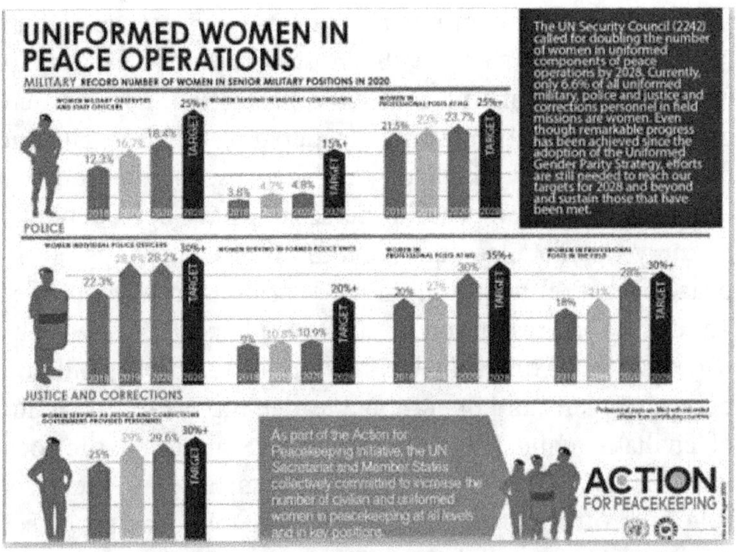

Source: https://peacekeeping.un.org/en/infographics

Specific targets for the end of 2021, as given on the UNPO web pages, were:

> ➢ UN Military Experts on Mission and Staff Officers: 18% women. As of Nov 2021, Ghana had deployed over 1/3ʳᵈ (33.33%) of its contribution from female

participants.

➤ The target for December 2021 for contingents was 8% women soldiers. Ghana again with 14.89% followed by Ethiopia with 11% are amongst the TCC contributors of more than 1000 peacekeeping troops.

➤ For top five deployments of more than 9,000 peacekeepers, female percentage amongst the uniformed soldiers and police persons hovers around 7 to 8%, which remained below the targets.

➤ The gender Statistics at end of December 2021 is given in the table:

PK Mission (With deployment of more than 9000 uniformed personnel)	Total Military	Female troops	Total UNPOL	Women police persons	Percentage of all uniformed personnel
UNMISS (South Sudan)	845	13896	1416	416	8.2%
MONUSCO (Congo)	13078	752	1643	319	7.2%
MINUSMA (Mali)	12419	554	1744	272	5.8%
MINUSCA (Central African Republic)	11453	756	2377	308	7.7%
UNIFIL (Lebanon)	9629	645	0	0	6.7%

Source: *https://peacekeeping.un.org/sites/default/files/07_gender_ statistics_45_dec_2021.pdf*

Undoubtedly, the UNPOs are deploying more women military personnel but numbers are still very low. They serve as leaders, military observers, staff officers and troops. They are carrying out all operations including patrols, flying helicopters, medical outreach, and many engineering tasks like clearing minefields. As of January 2018, women made up 9.67% of the military members contracted in the Office of Military Affairs, UNHQ. Women Military Observers (MOs) and Staff Officers (SOs) made up 8.2% in January 2018. The number of women serving in contingents was extremely low in 2018 at 3.9%[2]. By the end of 2021, there were 67,409 military personnel in UNPOs, out of which 4332 were female troops. This constituted 6.4%, a rise from 2.3% in 2010[3].

Similarly, UNPOL has very critical roles in UNPOs at the community level. Promotion of rule of law, administration of justice and building institutions of governance in conflict-affected countries could be their critical contributions. Their role in improving access of local women and children to law enforcement agencies and becoming a role-models to women and girl has been recognized across the international communities. By December 2021, UNPOL had 7676 personnel with 1418 female police officers, thus a good 18.4% representation. This increased from 9.6% in 2010[4].

The statistics given on the UN Web page reflects that the total peacekeepers including experts on the UNPO missions as on 31 Dec 2021 were 75,085. Out of this, 5750 were female peacekeepers making it to 7.56% of the total peacekeepers. In spite of slow progress, the representation has been a reasonable success as is seen in the following infographics.

---

2   https://peacekeeping.un.org/sites/default/files/uniformed-gender-parity-2018-2028.pdf

3   https://peacekeeping.un.org/sites/default/files/dec10.pdf

4   ibid

From 20 female peacekeepers from 1957 to 1989; the number has risen to 5750 by the end of December 2021. Seven leaders at SRSG level also shows a growing role as head of missions. Out of 52 UNPOL units, 32 have mixed gender composition.

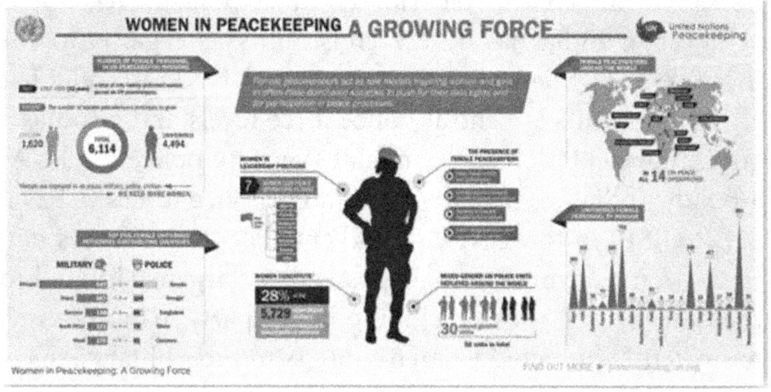

Source: https://peacekeeping.un.org/en/infographics

India's Contribution

The contribution of Indian peacekeepers has been commendable and acknowledged the world over. Indian peacekeepers participate in the most difficult missions where many capable nations and specially the global North shy away for fear of political reasons as well casualties. India with 5598 uniformed personnel was the third highest contributor to UNPOs as on 31 Jan 2022, only after sub-continent's neighbours - Bangla Desh and Nepal. India had 47 experts, 167 UNPOL personnel, 115 staff officers and 5269 troops in the UNPO missions as on 31 January 2022[5]. 16% of its experts and staff officers as female members[6], however at military

---

5   https://peacekeeping.un.org/sites/default/files/01_contributions_to_un_peacekeeping_operations_by_country_and_post_46_jan_22.pdf

6   https://peacekeeping.un.org/sites/default/files/operational_effect_and_women_peacekeepers-31-oct_2021.pdf

contingent's level, there is only 1% female representation. Bangladesh with 2.9% and Nepal with 3.8% have a better representation.

India has been the torchbearer in fielding all-women police contingents in Liberia. While at police level, this is achievable, India has severe constraints as regards to the increase in female military troops in any UNPOs. India has all women units at central police force levels and also has a good representation of women at the state police levels. As a policy, India has fielded only central police forces (CRPG, ITBP, CISF) in the UNPOs and kept state police forces out. In the Armed forces, female presence is largely confined to the officer level, thus precluding larger participation. Army has recently inducted women soldiers in the Military Police, who can be deployed on a limited role. Indian units are generally from the Infantry with some participation from the Armoured Corps and mechanized Infantry. These units have no female soldiers or officers, thus this goal of increasing female representation will continue to elude for some times to come.

Conclusion

With increasing emphasis on protection of civilians, and most victims of conflicts being women and children; the role of female peacekeepers has been recognized by the UN, member states and all P/TCCs. There is gradual increase in female participation and that augurs well for the effectiveness to peace operations. India also needs to devise innovative ways to increase female participation in some of the mission components, where there is larger presence of women in armed forces and police forces. Military observers, staff officers and police monitors could be some of these areas.

Reminiscences on the Evolution of the Women Peace and Security Agenda: The Backstory

Ambassador Lakshmi Puri[1]

The Backstory

The Women, Peace and Security Agenda (WPS) propounded in United Nations Security Council Resolution 1325 of 2000, provides a holistic approach to peace and security with four main pillars: - women's voice, participation and leadership, their special role in conflict prevention, the importance of protection of women and girls during conflict and ensuring that the post-conflict relief, recovery and reconstruction efforts meet the needs of women and girls and engage their agency and Build Back Better in terms of gender-equal governance, economy and society. WPS addresses the gender dimensions of armed conflict; the undervalued and underutilised contributions that women make to conflict prevention, peace-making and conflict resolution, peacekeeping and peacebuilding. It stresses the importance of ensuring women's equal and full participation as active agents at all levels of peace and security policy and action; and in the continuum of peace to development.

---

1   Former Assistant Secretary General UN and Deputy Executive Director, UN Women.

UN Women's Signal Role

WPS has been one of the five thematic pillars of the first global organization created to promote gender equality and women's empowerment - UN Women - since 2011. As I built up the organization ground up and set its strategic compass, I had the privilege of contributing to strengthening the WPS Agenda and its implementation for 7 years as Assistant Secretary-General UN and Deputy Executive Director, UN Women, in seminal ways. We built robust norms and standards through intergovernmental bodies especially the UN Security Council (UNSC). We pushed the envelope on UN system-wide buy-in, action and coordination. We activated advocacy and movement building among member states, their foreign and defence policy establishments and among "We the people" and civil society. We developed credible data and knowledge base on the why what and how of leveraging the WPS agenda for sustainable peace. We tried to ensure through UN Women programs on the ground, that WPS becomes a reality in preventing war and waging peace in real-time for countries in, and emerging from, conflict.

UN Women has been uniquely placed to integrate the WPS agenda into its other four thematic priorities of Economic Empowerment, Eliminating violence against women and girls, Gender-responsive legal and policy frameworks and budgeting, and political participation and leadership. In addition, we sought to mainstream Sustainable Development Goal 5 on Achieving Gender Equality and the Empowerment of all Women and girls into the WPS paradigm, so that every post-conflict country embraces it and seeks to achieve its nine targets.

The adoption of UNSC Resolution 1325 on Women, Peace, and Security (WPS) in 2000 was a ground-breaking achievement for women's inclusion in international affairs and in recognizing their vital contributions to peace and security. Most importantly, UN WOMEN picked up the 1325 baton and ran a relentless marathon to give life, content, direction and meaning to this policy innovation. We actively engaged with concerned member states and fostered and supported the WPS civil society constituency to reiterate, deepen and widen the scope of the WPS agenda and commitment to implement it more vigorously and systematically than ever before.

The UNSC Universe of Norms

Thus, apart from 1325, nine UNSC Resolutions were passed marking the normative advancement of the WPS strategy and enhancing its impact. These include WPS Resolutions 1820 (2008), 1888 (2008), 1889 (2009), 1960 (2010), and with UN WOMEN support 2011 onwards 2106 (2013), 2122 (2013), 2242 (2015), 2467 (2019), and 2493 (2019). WPS provisions were also included in other country-specific and thematic UNSC resolutions. In addition, UN WOMEN ensured that there be an open debate on WPS in October / November every year and that either a resolution or a Presidential statement (PRST) be adopted to further recommit, clarify, expound and set out conditions for effective implementation.

Six Presidential Statements reinforced the ten resolutions. S/PRST/2011/20 welcomed the role of UN Women in the implementation of WPS resolutions. S/PRST/2012/3 (2012) stressed that sexual violence challenges sustainable peace processes and regretted the continuing under-representation of women in formal peace

1325 (2000) - Recognizes that women and children account for the vast majority of those adversely affected by armed conflict.

1820 (2008) – Recognizes CRSV as a tactic of warfare and a critical component of the maintenance of international peace and security.

1888 (2008) – Strengthens tools for implementing 1820 through assigning leadership, building judicial response expertise, and reporting mechanisms.

1889 (2009) – Addresses women's exclusion from early recovery and peacebuilding and lack of adequate planning and funding for their needs.

1960 (2010) – Provides an accountability system for addressing CRSV (MARA).

2106 (2013) – Strengthens accountability for implementation of CRSV resolutions.

2122 (2013) – creates stronger measures to include women in peace processes and calls for regular briefings and reports on Women, Peace and Security issues to various organizations and members of the United Nations.

2242 (2015) – Double the number of female peacekeepers in missions.

2467 (2019) – Reiterates how women and girls disproportionately experience human rights violations in conflict and post-conflict settings and are underrepresented in many formal processes and bodies in the maintenance of peace and security.

2493 (2019) - Urges member states to commit to implementing the nine previously adopted resolutions.

processes. S/PRST/2012/3 (2012) reiterated its intention to fight impunity and uphold accountability for serious crimes against women and girls during and post-conflict situations. S/PRST/2012/23 reaffirmed the Security Council's commitments to full implementation of all WPS resolutions, highlighting the important role of civil society in increasing women's participation in all peace efforts. S/PRST/2014/21 highlighted the importance of implementation of the WPS Agenda, as a cross-cutting subject throughout all UN thematic areas and at national, regional, and local levels. S/PRST/2015/25 called for accountability of those trafficking in persons during armed conflict and for steps to mitigate the risk. S/PRST/2016/9 encouraged Member States to increase their WPS funding including through more aid in conflict and post-conflict situations for targeted gender-responsive programs.

Through these and other resolutions and PRSTs and debates in the UNSC, we managed to constantly update the WPS agenda to also include the equally important humanitarian and countering violent extremism dimensions of WPS. At the same time, we secured a mechanism - the Informal Expert Group of the Security Council serviced by UN Women within UNSC - to constantly drive, review and monitor WPS mainstreaming and implementation in all key peace undertakings and missions of the UN. UN Women regularly presented reports to the UNSC. Through this advocacy, certain practices became standard, when a report was presented by the UN on any peacekeeping or peace building mission it would include a section on the progress of the implementation of the WPS agenda.

Engendering the 2015 UN Peace Reviews

I was convinced that we could not pretend to improve the way in which women's empowerment and leadership can help prevent and resolve conflicts without simultaneously influencing the largest review of UN peace missions since 2000 that was undertaken in 2015. UN peacekeeping missions (PKMs) are one of our most visible and valuable forces at the ground level and can profoundly impact women's lives. Similarly, we cannot take a hard look at the effectiveness of our peacebuilding architecture without putting women's empowerment and gender equality at their centre, both as an enabler and beneficiaries. Hence, we engaged with and successfully gender mainstreamed the other two peace review processes of the UN.

The UN's WPS architecture was strengthened with a greater role and visibility for gender advisors in PKMs on civilian and military sides and with UN Women providing inputs, guidelines, training, monitoring and on-ground support as required. Convincing the main UN peace actors and governments of Troop Contributing Countries and host countries was challenging. Besides turf issues, questions arose about how gender equality considerations could affect operational effectiveness for example. It was often an uphill task for UN Women to advocate on the "soft issues" of gender equality and women's empowerment when member states and UN agencies and their instruments on the ground were preoccupied with the hard, everyday challenges of peace-making, peacekeeping, and peace-building - that too with patriarchal national war and peace actors.

We worked to convince member states through empirical evidence, actual examples, case studies and data that women's agency, when deployed, is indispensable for peace. We gave support to Women peace actors in countries, so they were organized to engage and have a voice in peace processes as in Syria, Libya and Columbia. Our participation in the UN Secretary General's Executive Committee Meetings and Deputies meetings enabled us to leverage his commitment to mainstream WPS in the UN's Peace and Security Project.

15-year Review of UNSC Resolution 1325

As part of a 15-year review of the implementation of UNSC

Resolution 1325 in 2015, we commissioned a comprehensive study to make the value proposition of women's agency a critical enabler of peace. The Report argued that women as peace actors foster a culture of peace with sincerity and empathy to make a difference in preventing conflict and brokering, keeping, building, and sustaining peace. We flagged real success stories on the ground and showed how the 10 WPS resolutions and PRSTs should be implemented fully - in letter and spirit. We demonstrated the transformative potential of WPS mainstreaming to escape intergenerational cycles of conflict, create inclusive and more democratic peace-making efforts and move from gender inequality to gender justice. We invoked the miracles of women's agency, voices, and capacities as critical to local dialogues in incubating better policies and more equitable peace deals at national and international levels.

UN Women–Winning champions of WPS

Our close partnership with WPS champion countries of UNSC - especially the Western group and advocating with other members like Russia, China, South Africa, Brazil, Japan, and India bore fruit. We acted as bridge builders between opposing positions in the UNSC. India's support for WPS in the UNSC especially as the third-largest troop-contributing country for peacekeeping missions has been creditable. India was a pioneer and made history in deploying the first-ever all-female Formed Police Unit in Liberia and they became role models. A Female Engagement Team from India is deployed in the Democratic Republic of the Congo as part of the Rapidly Deployable Battalion in MONUSCO and it has also pledged an FPU under the Peacekeeping Readiness Capability System. Indian women peacekeepers are playing an important mentoring role for women military observers and government forces to prevent conflict-related sexual violence. UN Women through the India Country

Office continue to provide gender training to thousands of peacekeepers from across the globe to educate them on their responsibilities under SC 1325.

National Action Plans as a Compass

UN Women's successful advocacy and movement building for countries to adopt, WPS National Action Plans (NAPs) provided governments, multilateral organizations, and civil society groups with a context-specific framework to ensure women's inclusion in peacebuilding, politics, and gendered protections for women and girls from violent conflict. They enabled UN member states to translate international commitments on WPS into national policies and programmes. In 2020, 88 countries had NAPs on WPS -close to half of UN membership. Fifty-five local action plans had been adopted in 16 countries and 20 NAPs included a budget for adoption. WPS Focal Points Network has 87 members. Six countries adopted feminist foreign policies and 24 NAPs include disarmament as a focus area.

Gender Mainstreaming UN Peace Missions

Of the current 13 peacekeeping missions, eight have gender units with a total of 52 gender advisors and officers, UN Police has 15 gender advisors and 4 in military components. Female UN peacekeepers are deployed in all 13 missions. Three all-female UN police units have been deployed: in Liberia, Haiti, and the Democratic Republic of Congo. Normative frameworks on WPS have been strengthened considerably including through the "Declaration of Shared Commitments on UN Peacekeeping Operations" and the "Uniformed Gender Parity Strategy." International courts now routinely investigate sexual and gender-based violence. UNSC resolution 1325 is invoked to introduce quotas in post-conflict parliaments and governments to increase women's political representation for example. The percentage of women at peace tables or receiving reparations has increased. The peace agreement in Columbia has become an exemplar of WPS mainstreaming.

Gaps and Challenges

Despite advances in policies and rhetoric, however, significant gaps and challenges remain at all levels including a lack of dedicated funding. Any advance is often quickly reversed by the eruption of armed conflict or the rise of violent extremism. Progress has been slow on realizing the aims of landmark UNSC Resolution 2242, of 2015 which I had worked on with member states and which set out ways to strengthen and benchmark effective implementation of WPS. Peace agreements continue to be officially recognised despite regularly failing to ensure both women's full and equal representation as negotiators and experts, and through civil society, and without substantially incorporating women's human rights. Most peace processes have women's minimal presence and that too is an afterthought. Our peacekeeping missions are heavily dominated by men. The Afghanistan peace process was a poster child of this failure. The post-Taliban takeover must now become a litmus test for WPS implementation in building an inclusive, resilient, and peaceful Afghanistan, guided by UNSC Resolution 2593 of 31st August 2021.

Looking ahead

We need to mobilize and connect movements to build solidarity for women's participation, protection, and rights across the nexus between conflict, prevention spectrum and peace, in the development continuum. Implementation of NAP/Regional Action Plan that incorporates strong accountability mechanisms, sustainable budget, robust disarmament provisions, dedicated and adequate funding for WPS and grassroots women peace leaders and the well-choreographed use of social media to share reports, advocacy tools, infographics and other resources is called for. India has rightly contributed resources for strategic communication on WPS.

Partnership with United Service Institution

In 2018, UN Women in partnership with the United Service Institution (USI) of India and in coordination with the Ministry of External Affairs, Government of India, piloted a first of its kind integrated training programme which brought together all components of UN peace missions, the military, the police, and the civilian component.

With the objective of responding to WPS normative commitments and building capacities of stakeholders in UN peace missions on ending Conflict-Related Sexual Violence (CRSV), UN Women and the United Services Institution of India (USI) implemented a comprehensive training Programme on 'Mainstreaming gender in UN peacekeeping to end Conflict-Related Sexual Violence. The programme brought together trainees from the military, police and paramilitary forces as well as humanitarian actors from select countries of (SAARC), to enable inter-sectoral discussions and peer to peer learning.

Thematic subjects covered during the programme included gender principle and culture, strategic, operational and tactical approaches to conflict-related sexual violence and referral and information system, use of early-warning indicators, response to potential, impending and ongoing sexual violence perpetrated by State and non-State actors, monitoring and reporting, and the 'do's and don'ts' for first responders and the roles and responsibilities related to CRSV of multiple actors in the field.

Partnership with Centre for UN Peacekeeping

UN Women, in partnership with the Centre for United Nations Peacekeeping (CUNPK), piloted a special pre-deployment training course for female military officers in 2015. This innovative course has since created a cadre of over 500 women officers from 52 major troop-contributing countries and has been replicated in three countries including South Africa, China and Kenya. I have had the privilege of visiting and interacting with the CUNPK on this partnership.

The Female Military Officers Course (FMOC) includes training on a range of skills such as communication techniques for interacting with survivors, warning signs of conflict-related sexual violence, information/intelligence-gathering to identify risks, threats, and vulnerabilities, knowledge of child protection, and gender-responsive peacekeeping. The course includes tactical training components – for example, the detection of early warning signals that might point to impending conflict, as well as higher levels of domestic violence or withdrawal of adolescent girls from schools.

Since the pilot of the FMOC, the Department of UN Peacekeeping has coordinated with UN Headquarters and troop-contributing member-states to ensure that graduates of the FMOC are deployed in UN peace missions. Thus far, nearly 70 per cent of the graduates of the FMOC have either been deployed or are selected for deployment to UN peace missions. To ensure the readiness of Military Observers, UN Women, along with CUNPK and the Central Reserve Police Force and the Border Security Force in India work to train peacekeepers – both men and women – to respond to sexual violence in conflict and post-conflict settings. We have thus far collaborated to train contingent officers, military observers, and staff officers to recognize and deal with sexual violence in conflict situations.

It was gratifying to me that at UN WOMEN we were able to make sure that the UNSCR 1325 WPS Project does more than pay lip service to the importance of women's full participation in creating durable peace and security. It is a mandate that propels countries into synergy, coordination and action, and has also a bold vision and the political courage to see it through. This challenge has never been more relevant or urgent. Women's rights and women's leadership offer a path to peace and security sorely needed by a world in perpetual turmoil. We cannot wait until the next century for gender parity and equality in shaping and implementing policies on matters of war and peace. Programs of UN WOMEN and Indian peacekeeping institutions give practical impetus to this vital but unfinished WPS Agenda. I do hope it continues to grow from strength to strength.

Closing Remarks

Major General BK Sharma, AVSM, SM & Bar (Retd)

Greetings of the day.

I am grateful to Ambassador Vijay Thakur and ICWA to partner with the USI of India to conduct a series of webinars on UN related issues at policy and doctrinal level.

My compliments to Major General PK Goswami, Deputy Director, who is spearheading the USI UN peacekeeping programme and Major General (Dr) AK Bardalai for conceptualising, coordinating, and conducting of the webinar on **UN Peace Operations: Women, Peace, and Security**. It has very clearly emerged during the course of our deliberations on the subject that women remain central to peacebuilding and conflict resolution. In a conflict zone, the worst affected are the women in terms of physical harm and economic cost, and emotional trauma. In absence of men, the whole burden of running and supporting the family comes on women's shoulders. Women also face a major emotional trauma, as a daughter or sisters, or wives. The role of women in de-alienation and rehabilitation is very important. Women have to be incorporated at the community, NGO, Government, and the UN Policy and military observers' level in addressing gender issues. In its entirety for establishing robust ecosystems. It also very clearly stood out that today this representation is not very inclusive even the analysis of some of the conflict areas where crimes or atrocities have been inflicted on women; those case studies do not do justice to violence committed against women.

USI is connected with the office of our permanent representative at the UN besides policy think tanks such as the Challenges Forum, NUPI, Responsibility to Protect, and EPON. But we need to further widen this network. USI has a number of senior and middle-level officers as our life members who have first-hand experience in dealing with these issues. For instance, when I was in Central America, I was involved in disarming, demobilisation, and rehabilitation of CONTRAS which comprised a number of woman cadres. Some of them were married, some were pregnant, and there were others who were inflicted with sexually transmitted diseases. We had incorporated organisations from other American States, churches, and NGOs to ameliorate their problems. In mission areas such as Sudan or, for that matter, for possible future missions in areas like Afghanistan, gender discrimination issues are of critical importance. UN mandates and capacity-building programmes must be geared to mitigate gender discrimination issues. There have been incidents of exploitation of women in mission areas by the United National Military Observers (UNMO). More participation of the women in the UN investigation and resolution teams will minimise violence against women in conflict zones or otherwise.

We are grateful to panelists and participants, particularly those from foreign countries, to support today's event. We look keenly forward to working closely with the ICWA to conduct more such events in the future.

www.ingramcontent.com/pod-product-compliance
Lightning Source LLC
Chambersburg PA
CBHW061250140726
47998CB00006B/2176